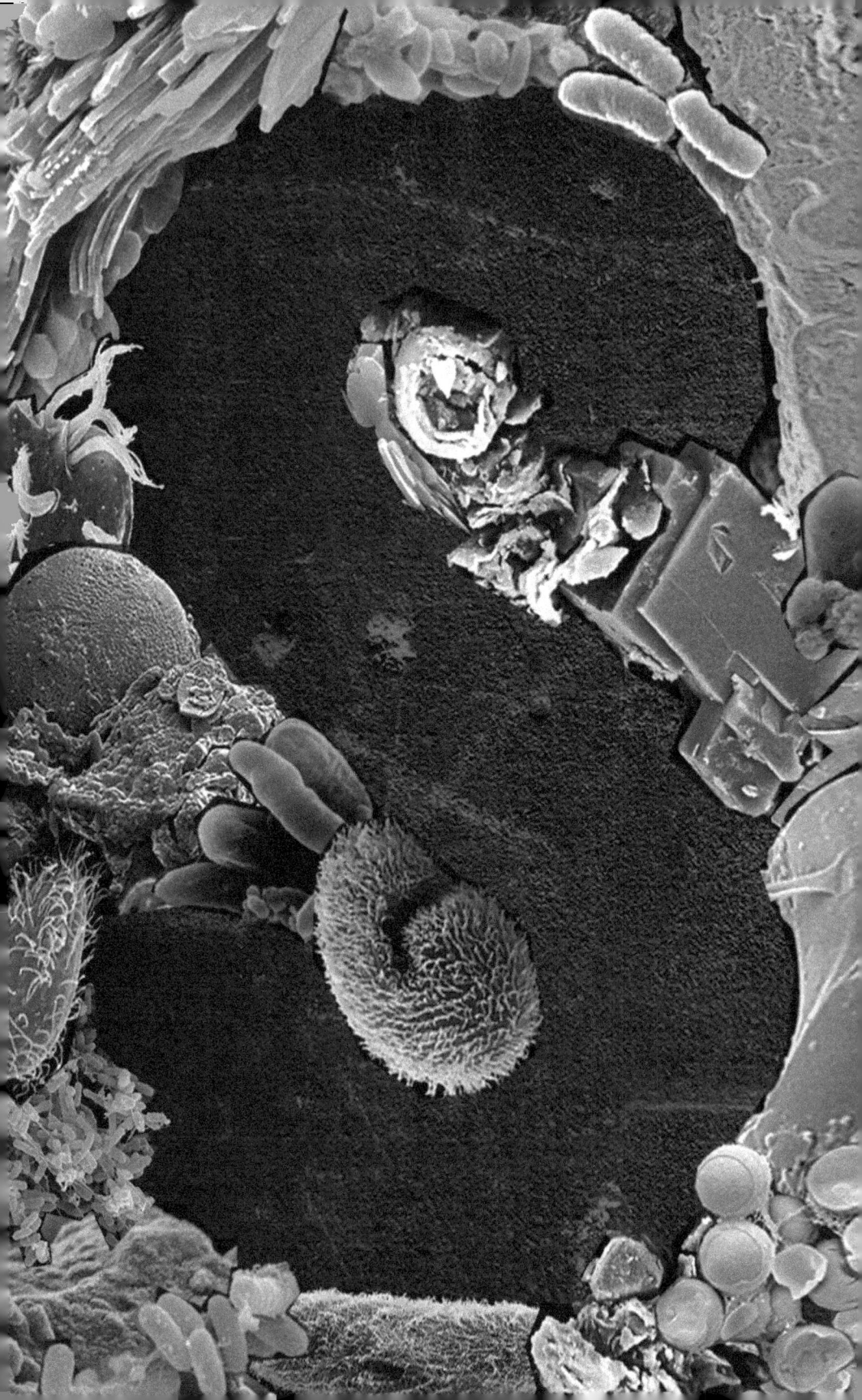

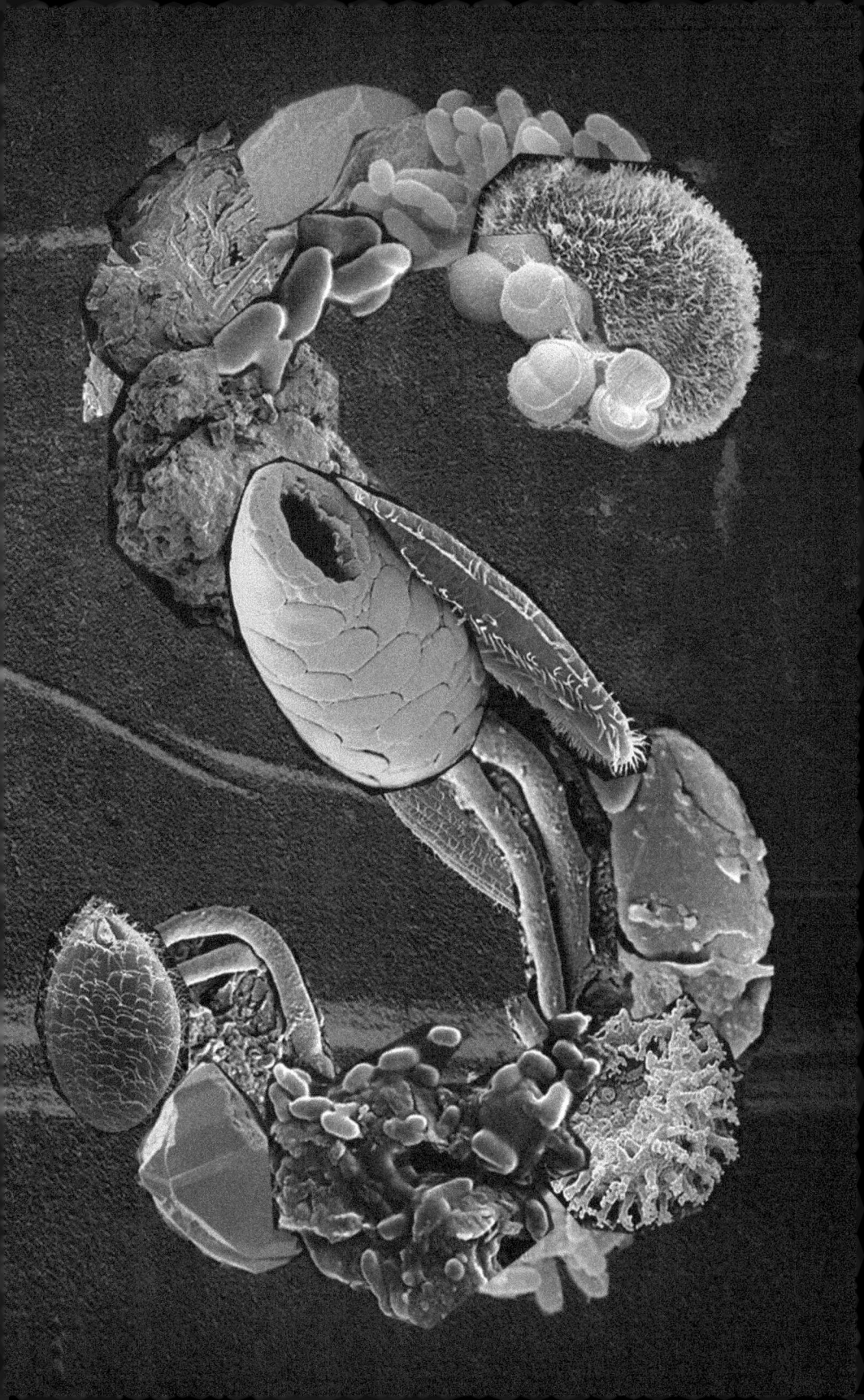

"AS ABOVE SO BELOW"

the SPIRITUAL SLOB

GREGG CIHANGIR MASUAK

Soul Odyssey
BOOKS

www.thespiritualslob.com

Author:	Gregg Cihangir Masuak
Artwork/Layout:	Emir Çaka Erkaya
Cover Photograph:	Robert Hayman
Cover Design:	Emir Çaka Erkaya
Editor:	Bronwyn Grantham
ISBN:	978-1-944068-15-8

Published by Soul Odyssey Books
A Division of Micro Publishing Media, Inc

Dedicated To

Ma and Pa,
who showed me the mystical beauty of opposites.

The Coozes,
who literally kept me alive along the way.

Nanny,
who belched and broke wind and left her teeth pretty much everywhere, and ingrained into my being the grounded essence of Love.

Michael Reitz,
the best friend anyone could ever hope to have.

Augustine and Sterling,
My darlings, I will love you for all time, just as if you'd existed.

LET'S JUST GET ONE THING OUT OF THE WAY

You're a Slob. You know you are. Otherwise you wouldn't have picked up this book to find out just what kind of slob you might be. You may be one of those people who seem impeccable in appearance and life-style, but you know that somewhere deep down inside you, some invisible something is letting you down in some way, and you're incredibly right!

That's completely cool, by the way. This book is all about how to turn that around. That dust hidden in the corner of your spiritual self, so to speak, that lingering in the crevices of your being. Better still, this book shows you that by allowing yourself to recognize and embrace your inner Slob, just how simple having the life you desire — inner and outer — can be.

By the way, if you don't like swearing, this book is not for you. Take it back, get a refund, put it back on the shelf if you've managed to read this far without forking out any money. I'm a gutter-mouth, always have been, and while I do try to temper myself in the presence of nuns and small children (with varying degrees of success) this book is a much-needed no-bullshit approach to spiritual crap, and I'm not going to adopt the usual tones just because we're talking about Big Deep Stuff. (More about this in a minute.)

I promise you, however, in payment for enduring my often brash lingo, that in this book what you won't have to endure is the annoying, constant paraphrasing of something you've only just read, or those wonderful quotes dotting every second page that, yes, are delicious, but are really just writer's filler-bollocks. You can get those in all those other books you're gonna read and forget. Or on the internet where all those other authors found them in the first place.

But what you *can't* get in those other books is getting down-low with the dirt and nitty-gritty of how to turn shitty into pretty. And once you start all that, you'll find there's a kind of element of fun in discovering just how hilariously clever you are in blocking yourself from being the person you want to be, simply by constantly leaving your knickers in the corner.

CONTENTS

DUCK YEAH!

There's method in my madness, and apart from the honest fact that I'm a natural-born potty-mouth (I've lost count of the number of times I've had to quickly and loudly say "Duck it!" around my friends' children in an attempt to make up for my verbal transgressions), there is nothing like the tool of cussing in order to shock the system into alertness.

Apart from my personal style of keeping things conversational, upbeat and engaging, the odd "fuck", "shit" or suchlike operates as an excellent mechanism — like a gear-shift — creating a momentary beat where the comfortable gears of your observation and assessment are retuned to the change of surface you are beginning to travel on.

So while I'm not attempting to be a Shockaholic, this book is deliberately getting you to loosen up your grip on those comfy-cozy bits of your environment that need mental and energetic re-visiting.

Our centuries of moral and religious training (neither invaluable!) naturally result in an ingrained bristling on the back of our psyches upon hearing these little exclamations — which not only keeps one from drowsing off and dribbling on the open pages of this book, thus crinkling the paper and ruining this carefully-thought-out and magnificently presented packaging (or, if you're using a Kindle or something like that, spattering your screen with an unhygienic drizzle) — but hopefully helps you to also revisit all kinds of personal concepts about language, thus opening a door to different thought processes, which leads to different energy movements, which again leads (hopefully) to the kinds of manifestations you've dreamed of — or at least a damn clean apartment.

As you can see, apart from my poopy-mouth, I'm addicted to very long sentences with a great variety of appropriate punctuation marks (and some deliberately inappropriate too!) — which is not just about method, but also a lot about how I think and speak. So if long sentences and lots of punctuation irritate the hell out of you, rewind to the prologue and follow the afore-mentioned instructions — or, hopefully, just stay with me babies, 'cos we got some cleaning and stirring and shifting and stuff to do — and some fun adventures along the way.

YOU & ME BABY

Now I know that there's nothing more annoying than picking up a book written by some New Age Guru living in the epicenter of energetic groovy-ness, so Advanced and Special you could never hope to attain his or her fêted heights.

You can imagine them, sun-soaked and sucking down their eggplant and soy combo on their eco-friendly terrace, rattling off yet another smug little bunch of pages as they benevolently attempt to steer your ignorant arse into positively transforming your life.

I totally get that.

Most likely, being the particular kind of Slob you are, that's not the life you want — and certainly not my life. Not at all. In fact, despite its dust and downright gritty grottiness, for me there really is nothing like smoke-choked crazy-making love-it-hate-it Big City living. The fact is you just want to make it all somehow run a little more smoothly, connect a little more deeply, and most of all YOU WANT YOUR LIFE TO WORK. Like a clock works, like an engine works, except with heart and that horrible thing that just won't go away, that we all know we should be paying more attention to: our soul.

You want it, but you don't want to actually put all that irritating effort into it. You've tried a bit of yoga, but it's a bit of a schlep to class and you really prefer movies and hanging with friends or cracking a cold one open and watching the game. Therapies and groups leave you cold; they're usually filled with bored housewives or those losers who look at you straight in the eyes and say meaningful annoying stuff, and that hour/half-hour/5 minutes in the morning of deep meditation feels good, but the dog has to pee or you have to pee and then the day begins and there you go! Dinner arrangements, a few too many glasses of wine and there go your plans for making it up before you go to bed.

Fact is, most of us just don't give enough of a damn to make space for being spiritual, even if we want to. We're aware of the clock, that ticking away of Life, and it all just seems to be a bit of a bore and a chore when you come down to it. Most of us are too busy, too tired, too lazy, or simply too overwhelmed by where to start amongst all those damn books we see on the shelves! We buy them, leave them standing there on the night-stand, maybe even get around to reading them a bit, and forget it all as soon as the cover closes.

And now dammit — here's another one!

Chances are you've picked it up, because you and me, we're both Spiritual Slobs. We want it easy. We want the wham! bam! of spirituality to impact us and just get the hell on with it — that wonderful annoying funky business of Living! Yeah!

A PILE OF CRAP

The good news is that just by LIVING you are a spiritual being. My friend Gaff hates me saying this. He feels spirituality is a pile of crap, and gets super pissed-off when I talk about it. As I love pissing him off and he loves me pissing him off, it's kind of a win-win relationship. And how spiritual is that!

The good news again is that one of the easiest ways to get your spiritual energy flowing is by doing something that doesn't seem in the least bit spiritual at all! It may involve dustpans, brooms, a vacuum cleaner, some detergent and a couple of hefty bags, but getting rid of the residue of your Slobbiness (and you "clean" ones will be in for a shocker!) results in energies flowing that you had no idea could flow, kinda like pulling out the hair and snot from the drain in your shower.

And then you can sit back and watch it all change, go for that beer (or a sody-pop or something else unhealthy), and see how it all works.

IT ALL BEGAN WITH MOUSE SHIT

So, far from sitting on my eco-friendly terrace sucking down my bean sprout whatsy and crap, I'm on my hands and knees, filthy as, well, dirt — human dirt — which is what I'm covered with: the dust and debris and grimy grotty sweat-soaked gum-smeared hideous residue of Office Life. I'm here because I am Flat Broke and scrambling fairly unsuccessfully to keep my head above water, because my life, frankly, has gone all the way to rock bottom, nose-diving into absolute Shit.

Years and years of goody-two-shoes loving-the-Godhead right-on-energetically-correct focus has still left me shoved as deep down as deep down goes before you hit the cardboard boxes and the tin cans, and that's no joke. Moving, cleaning, lugging, hauling, I am not making ends meet, but rather just barely scraping together enough to keep my phone on and shove a few bits and bobs down my gob.

Just to keep going I'm helping a dodgy acquaintance with his business, the business of going in when companies go bust (or equally dodgy companies do a runner) and clearing things out. Literally.

And, after weeks and weeks and weeks of this grimy soul-destroying existence (my hat is forever off to those who do this kind of stuff for a permanent dime, and we need to all pay much more attention to these unsung Heroes of Dismantledom), I'm on my hands and knees (again) with my dusty black garbage bag, under yet another of hundreds of desks, sifting through the lint and inches of grime, through the coins left behind and the paper clips and bits of melted chocolate and mouse poop (do you have any idea how many offices are riddled with mice and rats?), with the flakes of cookies and stuff you don't even want to imagine what it is — through staples and post-it notes that got away... You get it.

A whole pile of god-awful disgusting cee-rap!!!

Now, being a creative person, my mind tends to wander, and being involved in such an endless, back-breaking and quite awful and grubby task for sheer survival, my thoughts go elsewhere.

This is, in itself, quite a meditative state — being in the moment: picking up, dusting off, gathering, and yet remaining deep in thought.

And in this state, I start cross-referencing as I consider my friends and all the people I know and their habits, their cleanliness VS. what's really going on — and the various ways that the Lives they are living are directly mirrored in the crap they have around them.

I think of this because I am appalled and angry at having to deal with this company's residue, this disgusting, stagnant, smelly, sticky, hideous gunge. This blocked up, smeared, choking stuff that a vacuum and a weekly regime of efficient, clear, focused managing would have put a stop to.

Trying to numb myself to the reality of the ghastliness around me, my mind wanders eventually from anger and being grossed out into interesting little nooks and crannies until I find myself — unable to fully remove myself from my situation — pondering the AS ABOVE SO BELOW principle.

And I'm thinking: maybe, just maybe, this company — all these companies — would not have gone down the shitter if they'd applied a little cleaning fluid, a dust brush, and some attention to detail.

AS ABOVE SO BELOW

One of the Great Universal Ideas that has lasted throughout the ages, and for good reason..

WE ARE A REFLECTION OF THE GREATER SCHEME.

WHAT WE DO, WHO WE ARE, AND HOW WE ACT CREATES OUR WORLD.

WHAT'S AROUND US AND WHAT HAPPENS TO US IS SIMPLY THE COSMOS REFLECTING OURSELVES BACK TO OURSELVES.

WE ARE GOD, OR WHATEVER YOU WANT TO CALL IT.

WE ARE LIFE.

It seems so Big and Important, but in actuality, it's really very easy.

Everyone does it every day just by living.

HOW TO GO FROM WO! TO LOW

The As Above So Below principle can be a mind-splitting idea. Our farting, belching, orifice-gushing, hating-loving and all-things-in-between selves don't seem to resemble anything even remotely close to that rather scary, pretty big vastness out there.

It's tricky being a meat puppet here on earth, but when you start recognizing the fact that there's no difference between who, how and what we are and the things around us, it starts getting a whole lot easier and a whole lot more fun. Instead of striving and struggling with getting "up" there — by seeing that there is simply no separation between all those planets whizzing around and universes being created and the dust of stars being sucked into black holes and all that overwhelmingly beautiful (but frankly no matter how we see it just, unobtainable) vastness and lil' ol' us — we not only stop feeling like we're not GETTING it, we start seeing the results of how we create things.

Frankly, I like being my farting, belching, often brash self and find it impossible to really dig floating around disintegrated into some Om-ness: some loving, massive (and to my mind, though benign, rather annoyingly un-judgmental and personality-less) Uber-Ether Being.

This ego-clinging in the face of the Almighty Over-Awesomeness is exactly what stops us from "getting there" and, in frustration, causes us to totally slack off on the spiritual side of things. But there you go, our ego-clinging is unlikely to ever disappear, and in reality, I don't really want it to!

But if also, like me, you want to experience the reality that you really *can* have it all: the high of being low — a human being diving into the real, gushing joy of happiness right here on earth — then read on.

The first step in bringing the overwhelming Wo! of the Universe to the so-called Lower Realms of Your Personal World is the simple act of acknowledging the things around you as yourself — and cleaning up your act.

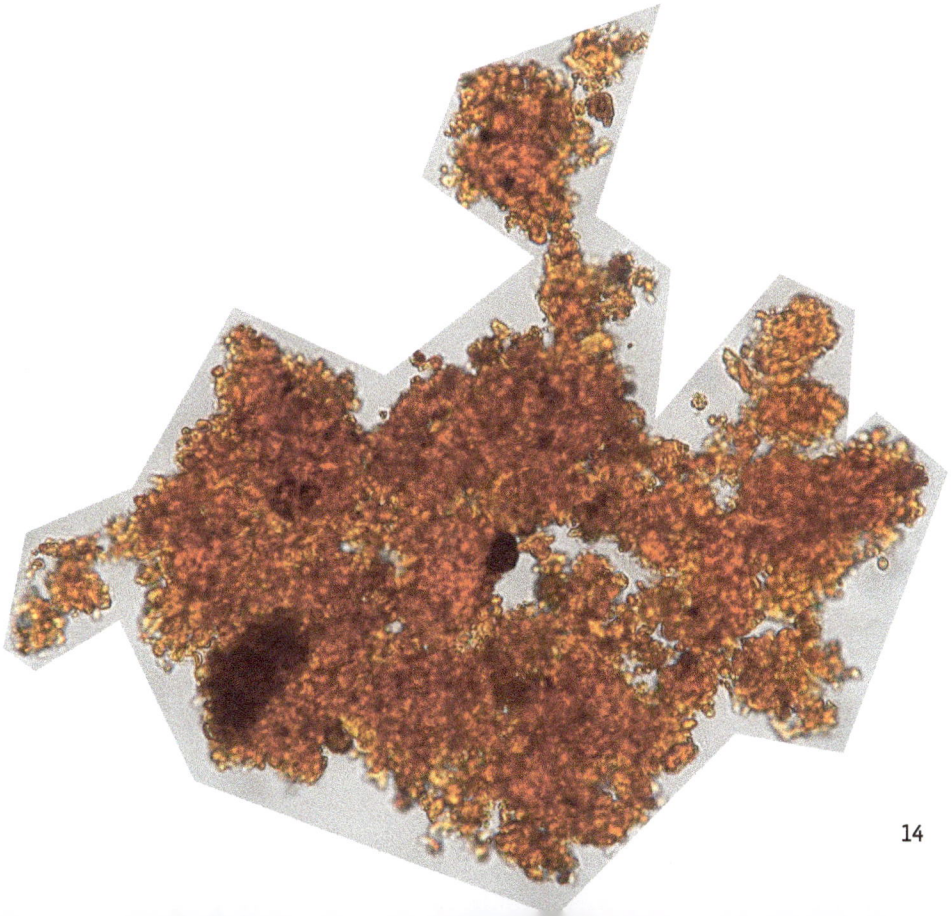

IF LIFE SUCKS
gET A VACUUM

Getting involved in Life is why we're here. Sometimes Life is great and we just ride and ride that wave until something happens and we're left dumped and smashed on the rocky shore. A lot of the time it's just kind of a mindless routine that plods relentlessly from A to B and we switch off and do whatever we need to do to numb ourselves — hence the attraction of alcohol, drugs and addictions, and self-help courses that suck all the money out of our wallets and get us nowhere.

Sometimes Life just plainly sucks. Whatever's happening right here right now, the easiest thing you can do to rid yourself of any present, past or future debris that stops you from riding the wave you want is to switch yourself on, plug yourself in, and suck the Mighty Beejeezuz out of what's around you!

"Hold on a minute," you protest, "What the hell does sucking up a bit of dirt have to do with my overall well-being?" — adding, with more than just a hint of suspicion: "Are you secretly tied up with some vacuum company?"

Well, I'd like to be, 'cos in this multi-layered world we live in, the cross-referencing of information — tied in with a little product placement — can be extremely lucrative, and I would really love to buy this super nice house I'm currently renting but can't afford to.

But really, I don't have the time for that kinda crap — I'm simply advocating shifting our lives, using simple tools that do the trick through intent and understanding. It's a much easier way of getting to the Godhead and getting the lives we want than attending an endless series of seminars that leave us feeling like gullible wankers or essentially flawed beings who just can't seem to "get there".

Sometimes a vacuum cleaner, sucking at the right spot for the right reason, not only makes your place look a hell of a lot better, but when you have the knowledge of what it's really doing, that vacuum act contains the same Cosmic Whammy as the Maker and you having several sessions of Canasta* together — and you winning.

*Canasta: *an over-involved, long, temperature-boiling card game that consumes all of your being and turns even the meekest individuals into canny, competitive, well, assholes. So renowned is this "game" for bringing out the worst in people, it was named as the cause for quite a few divorces back when you actually did have to have a cause for divorce.*

THIS IS HOW IT WORKS STUPID

It might be a stupid assumption, but I'm gonna take a stab at the fact that you're not some Bible-bashing nitwit who's been told from Day One that God is Love but still find yourself standing on street corners wielding great big placards dissing the people you think that God somehow, through his Omni-Ignorance, forgot to mention that he didn't include in the mix.

Neither are you some idjit who believes that by killing a whole bunch of people you'll get to fuck a bunch of virgins in the afterlife, cause horny as you might be, with an understandable but super-stupid vision of how you can finally get your rocks off, if you believe that shit you're dumber than a sack full of hammers — which is really a closeted way of expressing the original, non-PC version of what I'm actually saying, which is that you're a fuckin' jacktard.

It's easy to get angry about the myriad mentally disturbed actions swirling around this planet in the name of all kinds of Mighty Ideas Bigger Than All Of Us, but ultimately it doesn't take any kind of scientist to get that what spits from your brain into the ecosphere around you is a choice you've made, no matter how brainwashed or full of hogwash you are.

Yes, it's all about you — the person who's hopefully not wallowing in a conveniently created set of systems that allow acute Dumb-Ass-Ness to flourish, but who instead has picked up this profound (and I think quite funny, but that's just me wallowing in my own set of beliefs) book in order to figure out exactly How Things Work — and how to get to where you want simply by seeing yourself in everything.

Here's the thing: We are not here to be perfect. In fact, conflict — horrible though it mostly is — is exactly one of the Big Things we're here to kick about and examine.

Conflict is what makes us make (hopefully) healthier decisions; choose to go for (hopefully) better choices; and pull ourselves away from (hopefully) mindless follow-the-leader (whoever or whatever that might be) and into Follow-Your-True-Heart. And I don't mean some stupid-ass passion for punctuating the end of a sentence with a bullet, but that interior know-it-all-ness that hangs out behind all that.

Frankly, I can't think of a more ghastly vision of eternity than a bunch of saccharine-dripping harpists politely agreeing with each other as they float around merging radiant light energies with some endlessly drifting, hummy-sounding thingy binding it all lovingly together for no good goddam reason.

MANSUR AL-HALLAJ
A.D 858-922

Pu-leeese!!! That shit drives me frikkin' teaspoons, and if we can truly create anything, I'm gonna build me something more akin to Disneyworld, except with pubs and a lot of sex and stuff, cause that stuff is pretty frikkin' holy too, if you're not blowing up people in order to get it.

The thing is, Heaven on Earth is pretty simple when you start getting that you are literally fucking God.

Let me re-phrase that, for the sake of perhaps misunder-standing: You Are God.

Every frikkin' religion says this because it's true, and every doctrine reaching for some kind of advancement does too, but unfortunately, when push comes to shove, we're all really quite unintelligent beings so caught up in our ego-based bullshit that somehow this simple concept spirals off into   all kinds of unrelated-to-the-original-idea rubbish.

But there you go — part of the fun of living is having a laugh at just how complicated we tend to make things, and so here I am to spell it out to you, plain and clear:

God is Everything. You are God. So you do the fuckin' maths.

YOUR UNDERPANTS

=

BLOBBY THING THAT LOOKS LIKE A FACE

=

=

A DIRTY SOCK

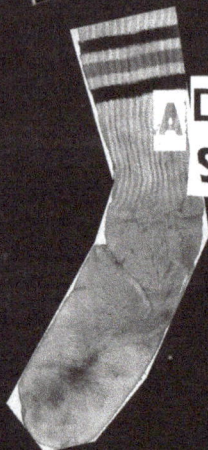

=

YOU

=

=

g ALILEO

=

NEAT CAR

ONE = gOD

NAKED DANCING COUPLE

$E=MC^2$

STRANGELY DRAWN CARTOON CHARACTER

STUPID WAR

YOU ARE EVERYTHING

Emir Çaka Erkaya, who less for his supercool name and more for his immense artistic and design skills, I've managed to snare — using tactics reserved for deep sea creatures conflicted between the choice of diving as far from me as possible into safety while at the same time desiring to fling themselves, fully exposed, onto my deck — created the cool chart on the page before this one, showing you exactly how it all works.

Just as Galileo blew everyone's minds apart by proving that it was the Sun, not our Earth, that was the centre of our planetary system, you are now at that moment when, instead of flapping your psychic arms like a maniac as you try to levitate up to Heaven — as well as paddling your feet hard in order not to get sucked down to the fiery flames of Hell (creating quite a lot of psychological tension, I might add) or whatever version of that you hold — you are quite literally, like God, *as* God, in fact *Everything*. And once you let that settle and really get down with it, you'll find a kind of immense relief you never knew was possible.

And instead of trying to manipulate situations and people and things and constantly finding everything and everyone, including you, coming up short, you can engage in a continual process of examination and understanding — at least on some kind of level — which changes the structure of everything, just like a mere observer can change the structure and nature of micro-particles in quantum physics.

And so the act of living in this world becomes literally an act of God (or the Ultimate Poopy-Pants, or Olivia, or You/Me/Everything, as I presently prefer to label God), and clarity becomes the key — the kind of clarity and energetic restructuring and release you get by practicing looking at yourself in your environment and seeing everything as you, thereby cleaning up all of our acts by doing so. Neat, huh?

If everyone in this spinning world immediately dropped their guns and switched off the detonators to that sure-fire highway to Stupid-Ass-Virgin-After-Death-Ville, picked up a broom, dustpan, sponge and some gardening tools and instead of focusing on what's-so-fucking-wrong-with-everything looked at the space immediately around them and got down to knowing that that space *is* them, then this Earth would shift so immediately and completely (in the right direction) that it would never, happily, be the same again.

In fact, I might get that going: an annual (then monthly, then daily, then minute-by-minute) Personal World Clean-Up Movement!

Look at Emir's chart. Study it, *get* it, fill in the missing details with the multimajillions of other things that you are, then discard all of it and just be Everything.

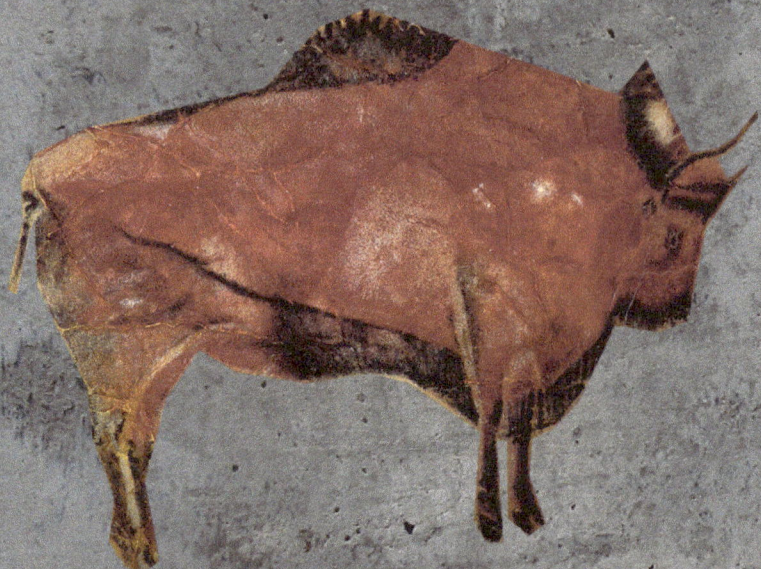

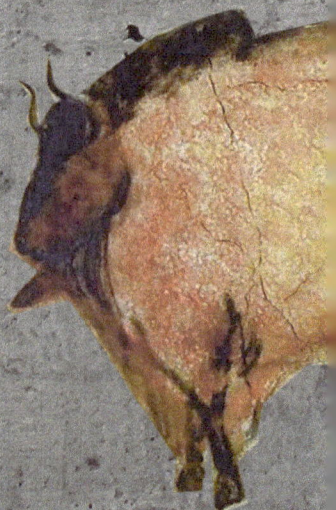

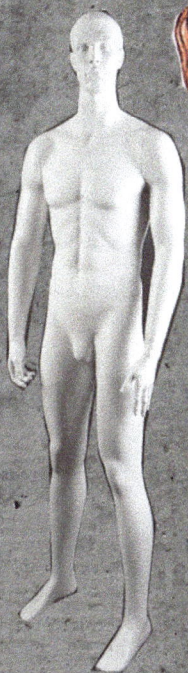

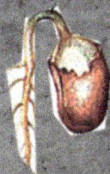

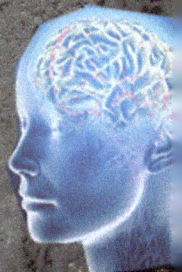

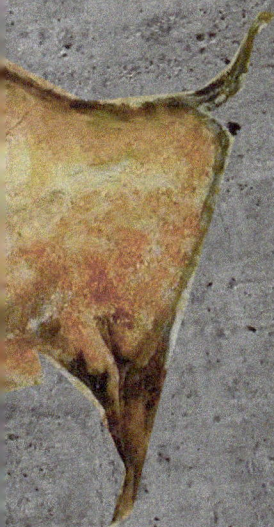

ET TU SUSPICION

While the expert Spiritualists advocate going straight to the Source (or God or Sheila or whatever the fuck you want to call that Big Energy Thingy Beyond/Around/Within Us), the suspicion we reserve — whether it be overt or hip-pocketed — for things unseen is ALWAYS, and I mean ALWAYS, within us. Suspicion is the very thing we need for survival on this planet, and it ain't never gonna go away — nor should it.

Suspicion gives us the edge against all those little landmines that make up our journey. It gives us an ability to make choices, create detours if necessary, escape from unpleasant situations, and choose the right book (such as this one) from which to gather the kind of information that we need to ride our wave in the best way possible.

Ingrained as it is so deeply within our primal beings, suspicion is the very reason that so often such magnetic tools as Affirmations* and Feng Shui* fail to deliver. In fact, very often, an unconsciously oppositely-energized affirmation or physical adjustment to your environment can have the result you *didn't* want, and I'll be talking a whole load about that one in a minute!

So you've been diligently practicing Feng Shui or whatever seemingly slightly silly practice has been recommended to you so you can Change Your Life For The Better, and things just keep spiraling down the plughole. Then you proclaim "Feng Shui (or whatever) is a bunch of shite!" while desperately hoping you're wrong about that.

And now you read this book and it says your Affirmations are probably having the opposite effect than intended!

*For those of you who have been assiduously avoiding any kind of New Age crap, Affirmations are the things you seriously say to yourself in front of the mirror in a valiant but vain attempt at re-programming your subconscious. Feng Shui (apparently pronounced Foong Shway, but who really frikkin' knows) has a much longer history, with billions of Chinese around the world and now you me and the Pope believing that the placement of certain objects and the physical configuration of your home or work environment can seriously affect your luck. This can lead to serious errors in decorative judgment, with the super-anxious energies surrounding those placements doing exactly the opposite to what you hoped they'd do.

"Now you've gone and slammed this idea in my head that this stuff's never gonna work!" you cry. "I'm always gonna feel like no matter how much I affirm, it's all going to fail. Thanks a lot!"

You huff off and slam the door, switch on the television and sink grumpily into your chair, popping the top off your beer and finding again, like the Slob you are, another reason not to shake it all up.

What I'm saying is, getting out your vacuum and your dust brush and your gym suit and whatever else it is you need to clean up your act requires a different approach to the one you've been striving to emulate. Because beneath every intent is a suspicious, primal anti-intent. This is like someone planting seeds being followed by another person pouring acid water on the earth.

So if you're nervously repeating: "I'm an abundant person, I have loads of money," and your situation is one of desperate debt, what you're really throwing out there in the Great Energetic Playing Field is "Holy Crap I need money and I need it NOW! I got bills to pay, my life is rubbish, and unless I hook some goddam ABUNDANCE quick-smart, I'm really going down! "

And Hey! Presto! Being the magnet and mirror that you are, you've set your *true* intent, an attitude of panic about as far from abundance as you can get, and that attitude is exactly the shit that's coming your way. More of what you don't want.

So I advocate doing the only thing a sane, calm and sensible person wanting to live the life he or she (or he-she, if that's your positioning) desires — the only thing you should do in order to move through all the energetic landmines planted around you: get a vacuum, plug it in, and with cool curiosity, start looking at those nooks and crannies you've never noticed before (or in some cases those disgustingly massive spunk-smeared arenas your dinner guests have thankfully never seen due to the flickering glow of dim, romantic candlelight) and, imagining your place is who you are (and it is!), get down to it!

The identifying of ourselves-as-our-homes, our offices, or where-we-are-as-who-we-are, or whatever, is the very identification us Slobs have been struggling with (and giving up on) with ourselves-as-the-Universe.

If you think this is preposterous, gimmicky rubbish, then think again. If we are the Universe (or Allah, or The Almighty Enlightened Everything) then we are just as equally, and in fact due to our immediate senses, more identifiably that dark patch of un-sucked, loveless molecules stuck in the corner of our living room; that unseen smear of barf on the under-seat of the toilet from last month's frat party; the yellowing grease-and-dust-covered Tupperware containers in the darkest recesses of our Lazy Susan; the unexplained brownish stain on the ceiling in the hallway as we are our own selves. Get it?

SUSPICION
Suspicion
Suspicion
Suspicion
SUSPICION Suspicion
Suspicion

SUSPICION
SUSPICION
suspicion
SUSPICION
SUSPICION
Suspicion
SUSPICION
Suspicion
SUSPICION

SUSPICION
SUSPICION!
Suspicious
Suspicion!
SUSPICION
SUSPICION
suspicion
SUSPICION
Suspicion
SUSPICION

SUSPICION
SUSPICION
Suspicion
"SUSPICION"
Suspicion
Suspicion
SUSPICION
suspici
SUSPIC
SUSPI
SUSPIC
SUSP
SUSP

suspicion
Suspicion
suspicion
SUSPICION
SUSPICION
suspicion
SUSP
SUSP

SUSPICION
Suspicion
SUSPICION

SUSPICION
Suspicion SUSPICION SUSPICION SUSPICI
Suspicion Suspicion Suspicion SUSPICI

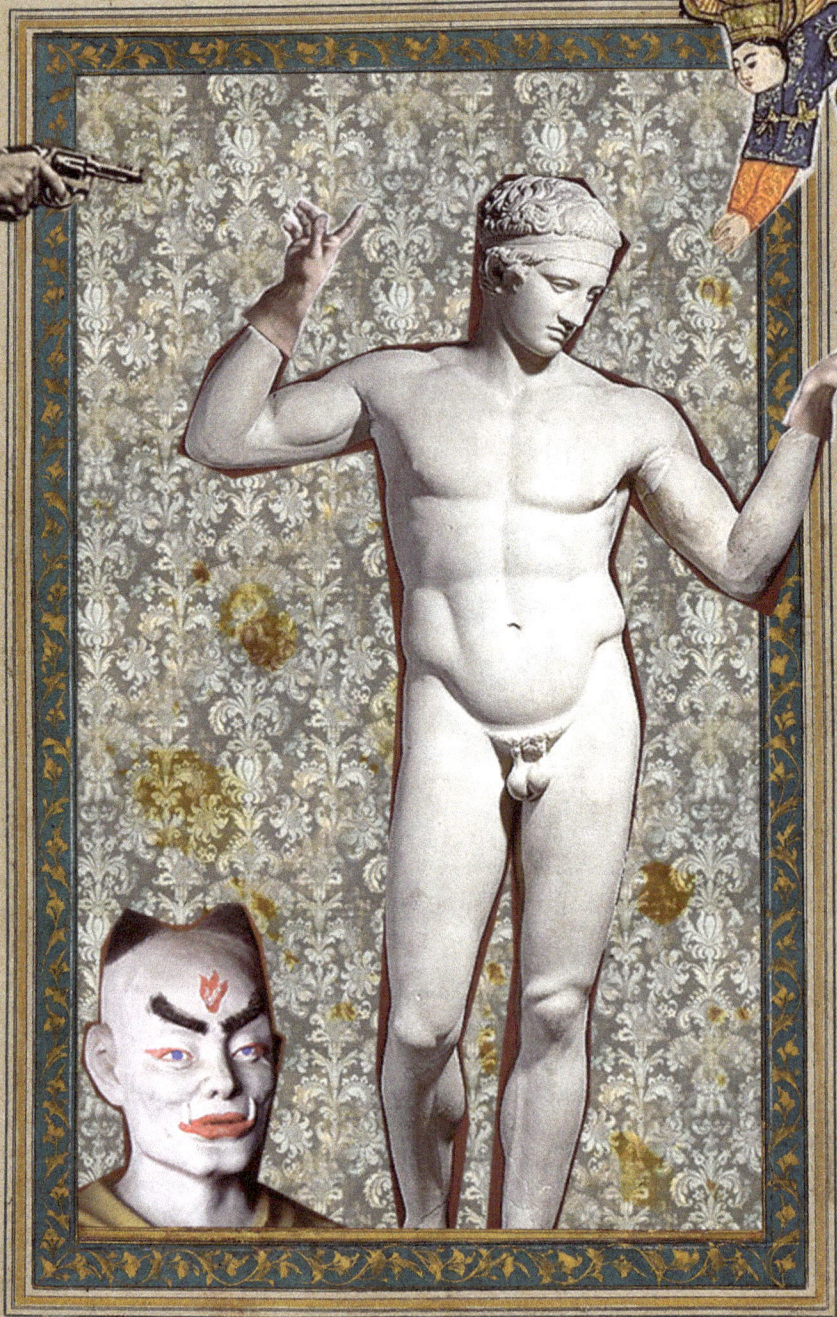

UNSEEN CHALK LINES

If you were to walk into a room and see a chalk line drawn in the shape of (you assume) a dead person on the ground, even after the line's been scrubbed away, no matter how much you tried to push it out of your mind you would never be able to fully pull the picture — and more importantly the feeling — that there was once a dead person in that room.

Whether it's your conscious mind or that part of you that sees all (and make no mistake, it does!), the mental chalk lines drawn around the rotten banana or the undies on the ground send ripples of neurogenic energy through your being, and that energy zaps around the matrix that surrounds you (and all of us), and before you know it there's a tension between what you're seeing and what you're ignoring, and as sure as Michelangelo thought of something and then drew it, that tension becomes a creation of your own.

That's why the simple dumb action of observing and physically erasing those things that would become mental chalk lines in your life is so immensely effective. A lot of books tell you to go within and change your world, and while they're certainly (for the most part) well intentioned, it's essentially a tricky and ineffective one-way road.

We're physical beings, and we respond to physical acts first and foremost. And while I'm not obliterating the wisdom of others, I'm saying it's a two-way street, baby, not a descending escalator, and getting down and un-dirty with the physical not only gets you the life changes you want, you get to sit on your couch and not worry about what's gone on there the night before (even though I can imagine!).

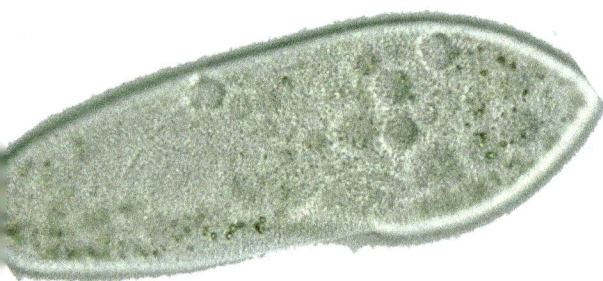

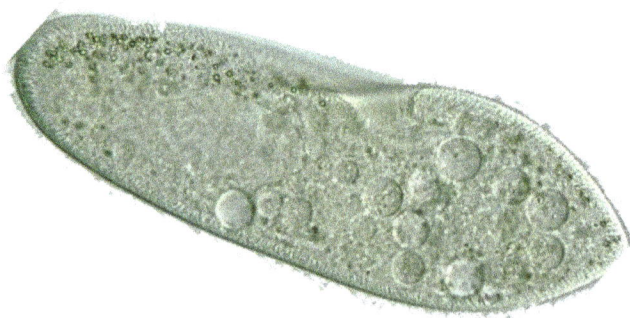

CASE STUDIES:
BULLSHIT OR SO YOU THINK

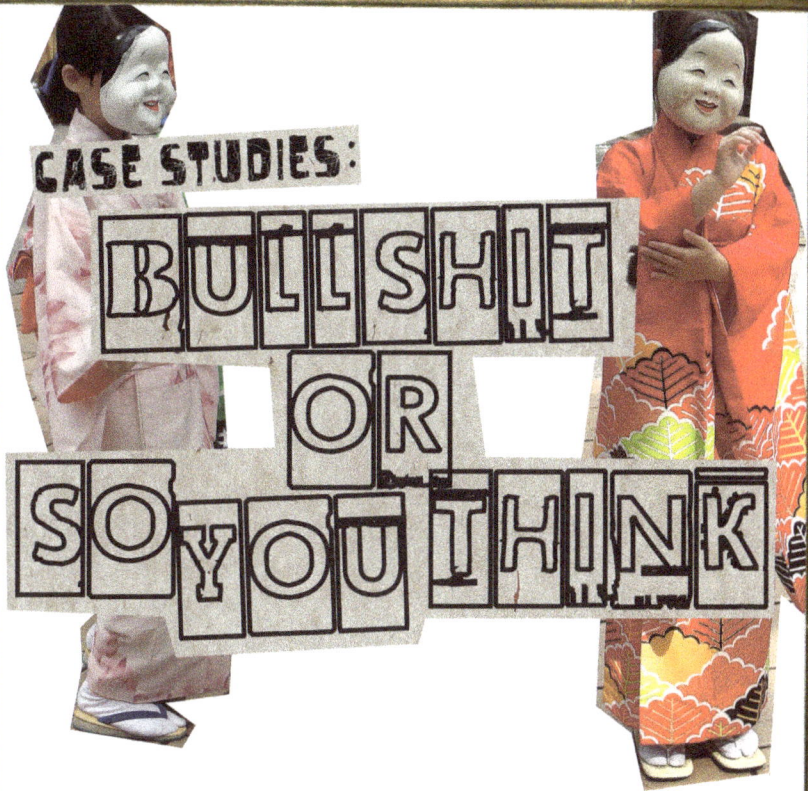

"Yeah, yeah, yeah…" You roll your eyes and start skimming the page real fast for something that might, like the implant of a micro-chip, WHACK that Universal Knowledge into your grey matter or that slovenly soul of yours, thinking "These Losers have nothing to do with me." (Like, well, frankly, I usually do when I read Case Studies in books.)

We are such specific souls each and every one of us, and while connected in all kinds of ways through elemental things — such as being on the same planet and having bodies made of the same kind of stuff all of our bodies are made of, and the fact that we all spend way too much time on Facebook and watching Reality shows and shit (stay tuned for the book on cleaning up your MIND) — and compounded by living in a culture of individuality (unless, of course, you're living in a culture where individuality is frowned upon, in which case, how the hell did you get this book? — and congratulations!), we tend to look at everyone's specificities as just that: their own shit.

In fact, so much so that most of us still, in the secret secret harbors of our beings, hold a bit of a torch for "I'll be the first person ever not to Die."

Which is all super-hunky-dory, EXCEPT our vehement individualities can only too often be just further smoke-screens that stop us from joining in the fun of shifting and changing and learning and thus becoming WHO WE WANT TO REALLY BE through the discoveries, the quirks and nuances (and the specifics) that others around us experience. Like the people in these hand-picked Case Studies.

Really, when it comes down to it, the reason friends and family exist (ok, some of us have fewer friends and family than others, and that's ok!!) is not just to share meals with or get pissed at the pub with or shag, but to interact and experience with, because fundamentally we are all intrinsically The Big Whatsy, reflected back to ourselves through others.

So while these Case Studies may not speak your oh-so-specific-specific individual language, each and every one of them are like little tiny beacons of light, like those little tea-candlelit paper bags lining the pathway to the party you've decided to turn up to — so turn up to it!

Read, and see through example how just maybe — *maybe* — those little hiding places of gunk in your own life are holding you back from being the shiny little Super-Slob Uber-Being you always wanted to be.

Not being a fan of Self-Help-Book-Filler, I've kept my Case Studies down to a few examples to sharpen your focus, and I'm explaining all this Case Study rationale to make sure that you keep the Señor or Señorita Smuggy-Pants inside of you from poo-pooing everyone else's lives and missing the point entirely. Besides that, there are as many Case Studies as there are people on the planet, and I'm too much of a Slob to bother telling everyone's story. I've got other fish to fry!

GOSH, HON
ON COOKIN
AND I'M ALL
CLOSING TIN
THE ANS

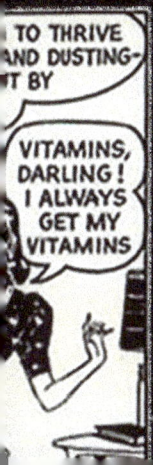

TO THRIVE
AND DUSTING-
T BY

VITAMINS,
DARLING!
I ALWAYS
GET MY
VITAMINS

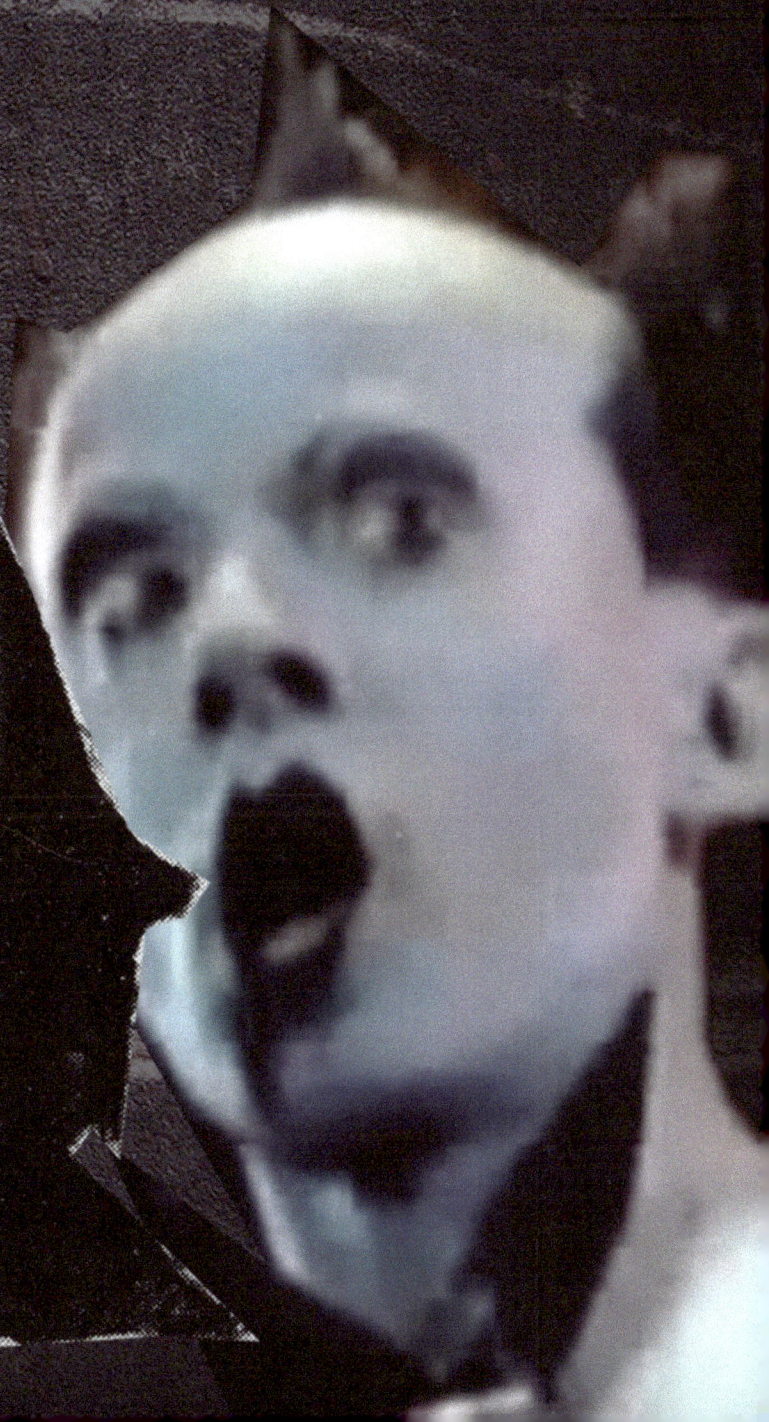

CASE STUDY

THE INNER ICK

Butch is a slob. Except he's the most irritating kind of slob, the kind who thinks he's not one at all.

He's the first one to point out the stain on your sleeve, the wrinkle in your shirt, and always says he puts aside Friday nights and Saturday afternoons for what he is adamant is his weekly "clean". He makes a big deal about The Clean, making sure that nothing — but nothing — stands in the way of his weekly routine.

As far as Butch is concerned, if it looks good on the outside then that's what it is, and that would be just frickin' dandy if his life was mildly terrific or reasonably fun or moderately engaged — or just even ball-park average, whatever the hell that is.

But As Above So Below, remember? Just a glance at the barely-brushed exteriors and a quick look at the mishmash of bits stashed inside their various compartments, and it is easy to see that the squishy-inside, armored-outside Butch is, like most don't-touch-me Crabs, just quivering at the thought of being turned inside out. Which is probably appropriate as there's something about those haunted Cancerian eyes blinking out from their hiding places that compels me to want to just crack 'em right open, but then, that's just me.

"HALT RIGHT THERE!!!!" you exclaim. "Is this about cleaning, or is this about your bloody star sign, or is this about who you bloody are?"

"Well yes, and no," I placate you with honey-like reassurance, marking that you've somehow turned into a bloody Englishman. It's definitely not about star signs (that shit's too complex to really broach here) though years of brazen (and misguided) Virgo-bashing by even the most honoured of astrologers has left me acutely delighted to have a tongue-in-cheek jab at their expense wherever possible and appropriate. No, my friend, this is about how your Essence — your Life — works. This is how *you* work — how your Life Force is directly speaking to you from your environment, a place linked completely into the molecular structures that comprise your body, your mind, your being. And your attitude.

Yeah, attitude man. Your attitude is just as inherently ingrained in every nook and cranny, every dust particle, every hidden discarded condom, every grease-spit-clinging-to-something as it is in the way you see things and the things you think of, combined with the things you don't see or don't even cross your mind.

The Everything and One-Ness of your personal environment is a dazzling, laser-sharp, no-bullshit barometer of your spiritual essence, which just as sure as pissing in a cup and having some lab techo give you the news, reflects back What's Going On Inside You. What's Going On Inside You in turn affects your ability to truly manifest in that unique Universe you are in — the Universe that you are in the same moment the centre of — and creating around you.

So while the exact details in these Case Studies may not be specifically you, you have the smarts and imagination to make this an interactive fairy tale with you as its central protagonist, and see that instead of having the long hair in the high tower and not (yet) having the Prince, you have the short hair in the back of the mini-van on the way to Spain, sitting next to the love of your life.

And instead of a long cluster of gnarly hairs shredded and tangled in the vines growing outside your tower window, you've got a shit-load of McDonald's French Fries you've never bothered to get rid of stuck in that little metal bit that holds the driver's seat to the floor.

So in this rambling manner, ducking and diving around each central character within each (true) tale, and including others along the way, you and I will begin to unveil your own story, with all its magic and forests of thorns and its ultimate Happy Finish!

Because sure as the Universe (or God, or Bambi, as you like to call it) likes a benevolent explosion (remember The Big Bang?), the release you will experience in the discovering of your own Truth — as revealed by the sickening (but to your own senses currently undetectable) smell of your cheesy socks — is the very orgasm the Cosmos is pulling you towards, the discovery that leaves you releasing, sweaty and breathless, that thick, self-protective wall around you in order to feel the deliciousness of the part of you that you've buried beneath a cascade of unwashed dishes or mediocre, badly painted portraits.

But back to Butch. As we've said (well, I've said — you've just been enduring my tirade so far), Butch is a surface kind of guy.

He wears a suit and tie to work (a uniform that hides his real identity) and doesn't like things to get too personal. Quickly, before you chew my head off, I hasten to add that there's nothing inherently wrong with a suit and tie. Or any form of clothing for that matter. (Well, actually I can think of a couple, but that's a massive segue into a whole other realm, and I really don't want to take that on — at least not at this juncture in time.)

But with Butch, his suit and tie is a device that enables him to keep himself, and the world, at arm's distance. It's part of his job, for sure — and his choice of job, like yours, does not always allow for personal freedoms of unsuited self-expression. Personally, I wore a hair-net in McDonald's for a year — a necessary though not particularly personal implement that didn't have as much to say about my own individual choices but more about Management not wanting my lanky, grease-filled teenage hair wrapping itself around the chicken bits and finding its way, subsequently, wrapped around some unsuspecting customer's uvula.

But with Butch, each and every job he'd taken had involved some kind of uniform — a not-so-curious choice for him to make, because as an individual, Butch does not like to be prodded, touched, scraped or examined. He does not want the world to see who he is, because Butch's fundamental beneath-the-surface belief is that he's filthy.

And he is! But not in that way. While being a pretty dirty birdy on all kinds of levels, good old Butch really has a heart and spirit of gold (and a deliciously soothing voice that should be featured on some radio program at night to lull us all to sleep).

In our struggle for surface cohesion, which is my fancypants way of underlining the fact that we have all been trained from Day Dot to believe that everyone we admire is exactly as they appear, the reality is that each and every one of us is a Rubik's Cube of disparate energies, searching to slot into place in our own unique way. Apart from entertaining you, this book is created to help illuminate those areas we think we are comfortable in (and actually are not) without fucking with those areas we don't think we are comfortable in (and actually are!)

Continuing! A glance around Butch's apartment gives the immediate impression of a modern and fairly tidy, well-kept bachelor's pad. A few pieces of furniture, unemotionally accumulated for sheer necessity.

Two framed, impersonal photos in the hallway give little insight into his character, as intended. Like the suits he wears, Butch's possessions betrayed nothing of Butch.

Which reminded me of my good friend Vida, who for years deliberately — and through the expression of her environment, subconsciously — kept herself hidden from "discovery". The discovery by others of her Inner Ick.

None of this has to make any kind of sense to the outsider. The reality of Vida is that she's a super-intelligent, stunningly beautiful, wise-cracking individual whose presence sparks up the room. But her interior vision of herself, as painted in the muted, emotionless, personality-less colors of her environmental tapestry, hinted at a deep need to hide from the world — to create a foggy nowhere-land in which no one could find her.

For the real Vida was in hiding in that deep and most essential — and to others completely inaccessible — part of her being.

As with Butch, Vida's apartment betrayed not a glimpse of meaning, emotion or personal taste. The photographs on her walls were all of her (and that's another whole story!), leaving no room for anyone else to infiltrate the safe harbor built around her — the protective insulation from an abusive and boundary-less childhood.

Examining Butch's place I came to find it very telling that, despite the incredible amount of mental energy put into his cleaning, you didn't have to look much beyond a glance to see that in fact, things were kind of, well, icky.

There was something quite different going on in Butch's world — something his environment was clearly indicating he did not want to reveal. So it wasn't much of a shock to discover that instead of the cleaning he was so adamant was crucial to his Friday and Saturday routine, most of his Fridays and Saturdays — and pretty much every day of the week — were spent dragging (and exacerbating) his sense of shame and self-hatred through the grubbier realms of acute sexual addiction — leaving those edges and corners and underbelly areas of his flat to express the inner stagnation and disgust he felt within himself.

Now we are ALL inherent judgy-pants beings by nature. What's not important here is your personal stance on sexual behavior or preference nor your individual take on what others call "aberration", or how much or how little you think that one should focus on such things. What *is* important is to put on your empathetic hat and get into how someone's environment can really speak to them — or how your environment can really speak to you, if you'd only let it.

In fact, another way of looking at it is that you've created this very particular nuance in your surroundings in order to speak to yourself about the very things a part of you does not want to know about, but which need to be revealed in order for you to become the Uber-God that you already are. How cool is that?

Knowing that every reflection of us in our environment — examined, understood and cleared outside of our bodies with simple intent — achieves the same effect within ourselves saves us not only the bus fare to the Buddhist Centre (they're always so far away!), but hours trawling the internet for unsatisfying distractions, thus additionally saving our brains and bodies from harmful rays and being overloaded with useless information. It's a Win-Win!

While the porn industry was flourishing under Butch's insatiable browsing, no number of unsafe-sex clubs, drugs or alcohol could provide the numbing of a heart essentially yearning for connection that was at the same time doing everything in its power to disenable that to happen. If he had looked at his own simple surroundings, he would have found clues leading to the elimination of Ick surrounding his being that he so longed for.

This particular example is of interest, not just due to the immensity of the problem involved, but to show how within one tiny microcosm — a small and apparently tidy bachelor's apartment — you can build such an array of mirrors to scream "Help!" to yourself. And just how easy it is, once found, that your inner workings can be cleared.

Butch's bedroom — what should have been a living symbol of rest, intimacy, self-healing and dreams — was a sterile affair. Well, sterile in feeling, at least. Just as Butch held himself and his emotions apart from the rest of the world, his "inner sanctum" was colourless and devoid of any show of sensitivity, sensuality, or self-nourishing.

Despite his protestations of cleanliness, beneath his bed was an inch-thick, blackened heap of gunk that had, in the 4 years he had lived there, never been broached, while everywhere in the flat the edges of the carpet had never been touched. This icked-up boundary was like Butch's own self-protective shield, keeping the world from discovering the ugliness that Butch believed in his soul was him.

Of course it's much easier to see from the outside in, and even grounded Uber-Knowing Virgos such as myself can be bewilderingly prone to the quirky motions of shadowy self-subterfuge by way of weeds growing in the entrance way that undermine the healthy bloom and blossom of our physical bodies, or windows so spackled with rain and city grime that our outside vision of the world can only be, likewise, distorted.

When you start looking at your world through the As Above So Below principle, it's important that you treat it as a game, as fun, so that in the midst of unpicking the wool that surrounds you, you don't self-harm. It's easy to beat ourselves up, but that in itself is a clever little ruse, which by surrounding ourselves with the myriad bullshit voices of our pasts and presents, enables a different kind of foggy distraction into the midst. What we want to do is observe, understand, shift or eliminate, add or augment — according to what we find and what we feel.

While it sounds simplistic (and kind of is), the first step towards Butch's dramatic, subsequent progress as a happy human being who felt connected with the world and good about revealing himself, lay in attacking the gunk in his environmental britches — and by him being brave enough to declare his identity within his own space.

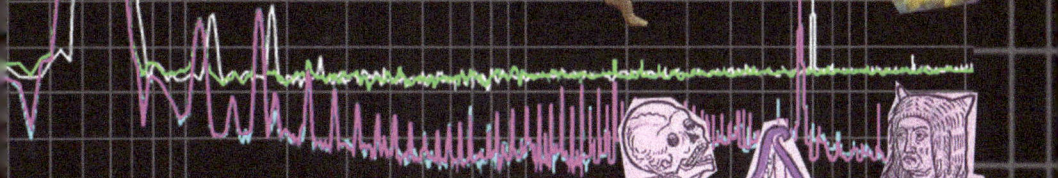

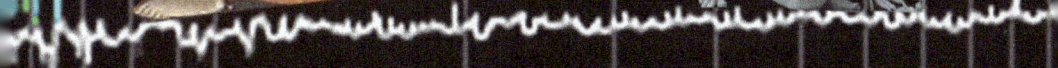

The broad strokes that smashed open Butch's palace gates, so to speak, came through the painting of gutsy, earthy colors on the living room walls and passionate deep red in the bedroom.

Textures replaced blandness and one bold, huge painting of the dog he loved so much was displayed proudly in the heart of his home.

And while all this sounds like so much Feng Shui bollocks, the reality is, when you get rid of the yuck and put in the things that make your heart — even against its initial will — cry "yippy kay-o kay-ay!!!" (or however the hell you spell that), you can literally feel your nipples tingle with the new-fangled, well-aligned energy you've pulled into your Universe.

The porn industry is suffering and liquor sales are down at the clubs, but Butch is travelling the world, engaged to the love of his life, showing his squishy bits, and super-digging who he is.

Sometimes a dog portrait is all you need.

CASE STUDY

SMUDGY SPECS FOR THE DRAMA QUEEN

My delightfully acerbic, ouch-smart and superlovely editor and pal, Bronwyn, upon reading my initial rant on Aquarians in this chapter, threatened to burn the entire manuscript of this book and sink both the ashes of it — and me — to the bottom of the ocean, which, of course, is soooo very Scorpionic of her.

But having grown up within a family of three Aquarians, I must say I hold firm on the matter, bewildered as I am by an entire clan so profoundly qualified to expertly navigate and indeed master this tricky little planet while remaining intent on doing so through such foggy lenses that it would make it impossible for them to back out of a driveway, let alone take on the challenge of being the rightful heirs to a whole New Age.

And while I smugly sit here, wielding my astute Virgo-ness over all, I hasten to add that no-one is simply one thing or the other, and that's the beauty of it all — us shiny diamondesque facets just love to irritate and niggle and nudge and cajole one another, recognizing, as we ultimately do, that we are all reflecting each other back to one another, and taking on major or minor roles from those people we love or hate or ignore — or shining our light back on ourselves through the very objects we place around us.

It's curious what people pull into their homes by choice — objects that either uplift them and the space around them or bolster areas of themselves best left unsupported, thus energetically undermining the very things they long for. Equally curious are those things that find their way to us!

So here I find myself living at the edge of the river on a private island in the middle of the Thames with the lovely but koo-koo-for-cocopops Coco — a talented writer, chef and, yes, Aquarian, whose personality is like that first pop of a cava cork: fresh and filled with the promise of delight and just a bit of naughtiness. (You're probably super impressed right now at just how cool my friends' names are — unfortunately they're really the same Bobs and Sharons as everyone else, but as they've threatened to kick my butt if I reveal their true identities, if I'm gonna make up new names for my friends, they sure as hell ain't gonna be Bob or Sharon.)

Coco's house can be found at the end of a long narrow walkway with a sign posted at the front door that states: "CAUTION! DRAMA QUEEN JUST AHEAD!" To Coco, it was simply a present from her sibling — one historically recognized Drama Queen acknowledging another by way of a little joke. But such a sign is precisely the kind of red flag we only too often live with, fluttering under our open nostrils, its message undetected by us, dampened as it becomes through familiarity and personal legend.

Being averse to the unnecessary distractions of constant conflict, I, upon arriving, subsequently suggested that the Drama Queen proclamation at the front door might be reinforcing more dramatic behaviour than was desirable, so the sign was begrudgingly relegated to the inside of the hall closet. But one can never just shove a Gremlin into the dark (especially begrudgingly) and expect it to be silent. Needless to say, the Ugly D for Drama continued to rumble and mumble from within the closet, generating its energy from under the door jams and into the whirling whirlwind that was the life of Coco.

Despite her intense and very real desire to be a successful writer, that simple Drama Queen sign was, in essence, one of the most obvious of the many stumbling blocks hand-picked by herself (or in this case herself-as-her-sibling), in order to distract her from her purpose. And so, instead of writing, there was the constant battle with the tax man to waylay, and the various blocks that constantly detoured her away from her more immediate money-making ventures as a caterer and chef, resulting in a continuing onslaught of unpaid bills and the ever-shifting tide (like the Thames that surrounded the place) of whimsy from the landlord that left her unsettled and unable to focus. Then there was Coco's policy for welcoming the dramas of others with open arms under the guise of needing to be generous with her knowledge — her penchant for "fixing things" would make the most stable of us woozy-headed, let alone Coco the Aquarian with Big Visions and no time left to spend on achieving them.

"CAUTION! DRAMA QUEEN JUST AHEAD!" was not just a joke still hiding in the closet; it was a self-perpetuating reality that somehow had to be disassembled, because with the dismantling of any thing also comes the dismantling of its energy.

Just like the disastrous ghost-busting I was engaged in shortly after that (stay tuned for more about that one!), which attempted to remove over 80 years (and in my opinion, a whole lot more) of yukky energy, the putting up and dismantling of things — whether they be objects, beings or accumulated ick — is fundamental to the restructuring of our very selves. Who we are is an accumulation of what we came wailing and gurgling into the world with, combined with the myths and stories, the decisions and placements of ideas, plus the things that we gather and carry around with us.

In the light of the amazing manner in which we are constructed, therefore, there is no such thing as a meaningless object if that object — whether it be something we've bought, been given, or has simply "happened" — has settled its reality into ours (there being no separation, as we've already established, between its reality and our own awesome godlike existence). Unfortunately (or rather fortunately, as we now have opened our eyes to those brilliant indicators that surround us), we often ignore the very things that, if shifted or discarded or changed into something more positively meaningful would be the very conduits to the Gateway of our Brilliance.

Which is why, instead of looking at the rancid, festering boogers collecting in the corners of our homes and sucking them up with a powerful implement, we tend to look at the biggest object in the room — our partners, husbands, wives — and point at them and say "You!", thus leading to an expensive and messy divorce, when the cheaper and less exhausting method would be to take responsibility, keep our loved ones, buy a vacuum bag, and get rid of the boogers instead.

I'm going to qualify that last statement by adding that sometimes the partner, wife, or husband *is* the booger we need to get rid of — and that's fine too and sometimes a fair enough choice, but this choice is your choice and your choice alone, and like all your choices, you need to examine it and take responsibility for it. If you really have cleaned up all the other gunk under the bed and dripping from your stove-vents, and have read and acted on all the signs that are screaming at you from wherever they are seemingly hiding, your husband, wife or partner may be — just maybe — the last booger you need to clean out.

While the more obvious items such as that sign by your mirror that screams "FUCKING UGLY", may finally knock their not-so-subtle significances into your noggin, it's the other, less obvious stuff that can equally get in the way of

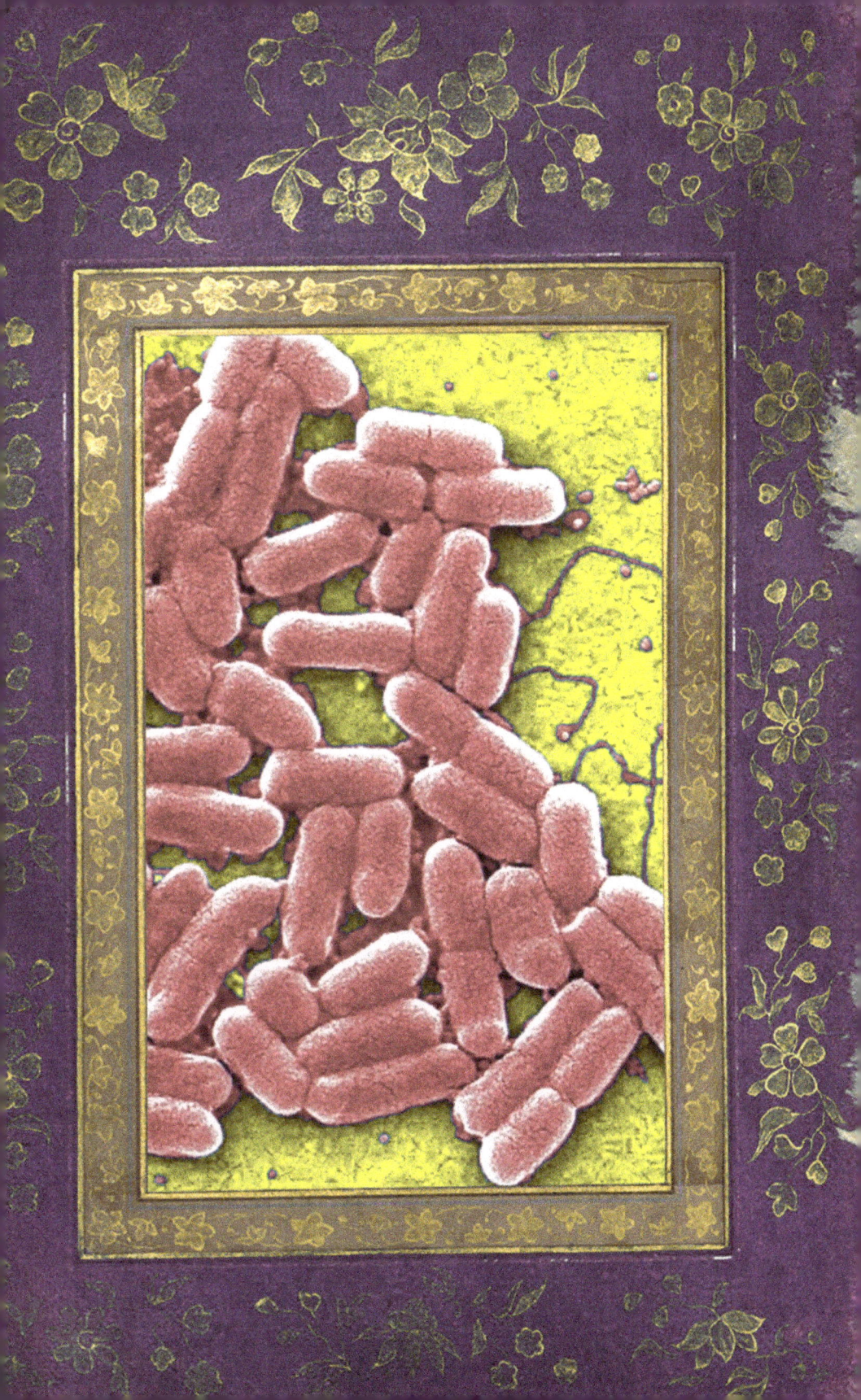

what we're trying to create in our worlds. By recognizing just how subtle this shit can be, a whole universe of shape-shifting, bullshit-eliminating fun is opened up to us. It's amazing how us complicated lil' ol' souls live on a multitude of levels all at once: the "me" who knows I'm "me"; the "me" who thinks I'm another kind of "me", and the "me" way beyond who looks down at "me" thinking (kindly, I hope): WHAT THE FRIKKIN' HELL IS "ME" DOING!!!?????

Befuddled by the endless commotion she'd unwittingly created around her, poor Coco didn't stand a chance of seeing the source of it all, what with the sheer volume of spider webs and cobwebs fuzzying most of the corners and ceilings, nooks and crannies of her home — and therefore her Self. No wonder her focus had a penchant for drifting off, her thoughts and dreams trapped like flies in a sticky stuck-ness that would drive anyone, let alone a free-flying Aquarian, absolutely teaspoons.

On top of it all, looking through her reading spectacles or trying to view the world outside through her dust-choked windows was like moving through the murky bottom of some deeply algae-filled aquarium.

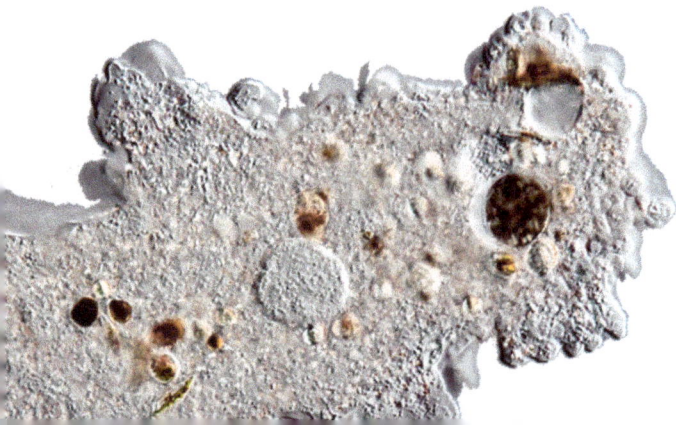

Along with the drama she invited into her life, Coco's grimy spectacles, cobwebs and grubby windows were her unseen warning signs to herself about the smudged and fudged pathway to her goals and dreams — a lack of vision stopping her from being able to view, read and write clearly.

Decoding our lives through cleaning is not a chore — it's a magic metaphysical door, opening to Who We Are and What We Want.

In that practical reshaping of those symbols that mirror the energy around us, we change our spiritual/physical/mental/emotional structure. That can't help but either fill up your tank with Cosmic Poop — or fill it up with the Extra Special Unleaded that enables you to get crankin' on the Metaphysical and Material Autobahn. So without getting paranoid about it — and recognizing that sometimes the very bits and pieces that piss on our parade are perhaps the much-needed hurdles our Supersmart Higher Essences created to build up our Cosmic Legs in order to leap into Awesome — respectfully evict your unwanted eight-legged freeloaders, polish up your glasses, and SHINE!

And get rid of that stupid sign — it's simply not funny.

CASE STUDY

STICKY BASTARDS

While you and I are fabulously and mutually growing in our knowledge and expertise of the shapeshifting of the minutiae of our chosen environments — engaged as we are in the happy re-creating of ourselves into the kind of Universes we want to be, with eyes and ears and senses all seeing and hearing and, well, sensing our way towards that Happy Never-Quite-Finished-Line — it's not a bad idea at this stage to pause and reflect on those energies that simply refuse to be budged. Such reflection stops us from indulging in too much hubris as we wend our way to our inevitable Awesomeness, but most importantly, lets us know when it becomes acceptable to throw our hands in the air and state: "Ok, that's it, I give up." In which case you and I can retire to the verandah, pour ourselves a lemonade, and ruminate on how exactly we were quite so brilliant as to get where we are, right here, right now, in the first place.

Committed to the Superfast Slipstream To Ultimate Cosmic Yahoo-Ness as we are, it's often hard for us Slobs to accept that sometimes — but not often — the very houses we live in and the grounds they are built on can be like belligerent elephants stuffed full of poop and refusing, despite whatever it is we do, to be cosmically enemized. In which case this has really not much to do with "us" anymore — at least the part of "us" that has no time anymore for the "apparently-outside-of-us" which refuses to play ball because it's now sooo very seemingly outside of us it really isn't a helluva lotta fun to play with, and really sometimes no fun at all.

Not that it's not worth a go: the flexing of our Bambi-Trixie-Greggy-esque Cosmic Muscles can be very gratifying, if it doesn't kick us in the ass, and one should never be afraid of checking tricky things out in the Rubik's Cube that is our ever-shifting, current, "here I am in THIS body" life. So with that in mind, one superterrific illustration of how accumulated energy from other sources "beyond yourself" can create an unexpected and unwanted, parasitical relationship (much like a battery being unexpectedly shoved inside a flashlight and subsequently finding its own energy sucked out while enabling the overriding instrument to illuminate itself) is when my good friends Cabby and Lange pulled me in to ghost-bust an extremely haunted house in Bel-Air.

Yes, you heard it right: I'm a bonafide Hollywood Ghost-Buster!

We were, on paper, the perfect trio for such an adventure: Cabby, a burly, take-no-prisoners, no-bullshit kinda guy who talked like a truck driver but had an incredibly sensitive core and truly did see Dead People — most often in annoying places like the supermarket or the toilet. Frankly, Cabby didn't want to have anything to do with them (he wanted to be a chef instead) and spent much of his money-spinning time as a massage therapist annoyed at having to yank the nasty critters and crapola spirit-refugees that clung to his clients' bodies off of them — never giving away the true reason why their neck and back pains suddenly and completely disappeared as he sharply banished the little bastards into the light.

Lange, one of the kindest people I've ever met, whose passion was writing, earned her way as a Dominatrix, and while her clients thought she was beating the shit out of them by their own demand, in alter-reality she was pounding the beejeezus out of the waywards clinging onto their energy fields, making sure the annoying creeps were well and truly thwarted from manipulating their host into playing out their nastiness in the everyday world.

And then there was me, Greg (then without my extra power-"g"), with my pragmatic and somewhat (you might have guessed) acerbic attitude to the whole shebang, my spiritual sarcasm the natural afterbirth of having my entire material universe collapse into dust. This punch-drunk suspicion of all things supernatural was weirdly enough contradicted by the sudden appearance of, in my home of ten years, a ghost-child who suddenly decided to take up residence and change everything I believed about the afterlife (that's a whole other story, or TV series, or something — get your agent to call me!).

The mansion we were brought in to ghost-bust was owned by a famous Hollywood director, who lived there with his gorgeous almost-actress wife and their two small children. Built in the 1920's, it was a legendary "Den of Iniquity" with the glitterati and the literati and those hanger-on types who crave, if not fame, sucking on the appropriate energy fields of the above, and while the infamy of booze-swilling debauchery and flapper-time hedonism sounded like wonderful Tinsletown dinner conversation, the reality was that, despite the current family's seemingly idyllic lifestyle and the external beauty of the house, deep problems lurked within.

When any brand of energy is repeated enough, it creates what I can only describe as a self-perpetuating cyclone of feeling. Which is why you can walk into a room and know immediately what's going on or what's *been* going on (and we should all pay attention to that shit, cause we generally don't, and it's highly useful).

So as far as the energy-field in this house was concerned, the party was never gonna finish. Nor were the leftovers of the party: the toxic underlying anger, the physical violations, and in my opinion, some very real skeletons under the floorboards who were bursting to make their presences known. As a result of the elephant continually pooping inside itself until its guts were about to bust, the place was spiritually reeking, and not one but several very entitled-feeling entities inhabited it, leaving a massive dungheap-stink of capital-letter CREEPY proportions.

This kind of Afterlife/Beyondlife Mob Mentality is a real thing, and it's up to us to decide whether we can be arsed to engage in it or not, cause us Slobs generally have better fish to fry than to try cooking up some crappy old cadaver just for shits 'n giggles — but as I say, we do like to flex, and if the engagement in such sport is invigorating, rather than resulting in us dramatically but uselessly shoving crosses up our fannies like Linda Blair in *The Exorcist*, so be it.

On the Other Side (whatever that is), where the Mob is a decomposed drooling mess and there's no one left in the club wearing a Voice of Reason badge, all that's required for that ancient, sick-soaked engine to grease itself up again is an appropriate meat-battery. And Hey! Presto! the party continues! (If you call a bunch of festering critters both once-human and never-human vomiting shit energy on themselves and everything around them a party).

Understanding Mob Mentality in our oh-so-easy-going Slob World is a good thing. The sheer buzz of enjoying energy, good or bad, zapping around and recognizing itself, is why crowds love to gather for the excitement of the Game, why walking into a sex club pretty much instantly gives you a boner, and why riots become, well, riots. But being sucked into useless energetic fields is the antithesis of what we are all about; ancient battles will continue, and Mob Mentality can only be altered by altering our individual energy fields. And that, my friends, is both our power and our pleasure — the infinite satisfaction of not attaching ourselves to gunk that just ain't serving us.

In the Bel-Air mansion, the uber-successful and wealthy and seemingly happy-go-lucky family found themselves resuming their own old struggles with addictions and the darker side of "fun" in that crazy co-dependent way that enables such tornadoes of energy to exist. But it was only after a few too many instances of their (very large) dogs being flung across the living room by the unseen nasties and the nightly wake-up calls from their kids screaming as a result of a particularly ghastly ghost-man hovering over them in their bedroom, that it was agreed that the party just had to stop.

Apparently, prior to us, the director and his almost-actress wife had flown a famous Spiritualist in from Italy, renowned for her ability to rid places of their toxic, unseen inhabitants. She had finally reached the room downstairs — the Epicenter of Ick (kinda like that closet in Poltergeist) — and soon after ran out of the house, screaming and terrified, refusing to ever return. So of course it seemed obvious to call three relatively inexperienced "Busters", such as Cabby, Lange and myself onto the scene!

In typical Hollywood fashion, Cabby had recently acted with the wife of the director in some TV series, at which time she had revealed her plight to him. Cabby, being a push-over, agreed to check it out, and had invited Lange, who was a shoe-in — after all, she was living in her ragged once-famous Deco apartment with the ghost of one of Errol

Flynn's dead lovers, who'd hover over her as she lay in bed, rolling his eyes dramatically and ultimately resorting (after her disinterest in his antics) to flicking the lights on and off relentlessly and moving cans of beans around on the counter top. Lange was as *au fait* with eccentric after-lifes and was as fascinated by their personalities as she was by the guys wanting to sniff her feet for cash. As for me, I was unemployed, destitute, and so pissed off with all things spiritual that I was the perfect "no it ain't" card to ground things — grounding being a very much-needed quality in order to have a hope in Hades of finally ridding that place of its Great Unwanted.

On the outside, the site of our would-be-Ghost-Busting mission was the kind of picture-perfect residence you'd see in a movie: a long, wooded driveway wound its way to the top of the Bel-Air Hills, opening up to a stunning Spanish Hacienda surrounded by lush gardens, flanked by an enormous lagoon of a swimming pool, with tennis courts akimbo and several guest-houses linked by jasmine-covered archways. But despite all of its exterior glamour, a melancholic atmosphere permeated the grounds, as tangible and as pungent as the infected gonads of a Namibian Wildebeest. Meanwhile, the inside of the place was a sunless, confusing network of corridors — a rambling labyrinth of a house that seemed to have a life of its own, seemingly dictating the style of its furnishings to its owners.

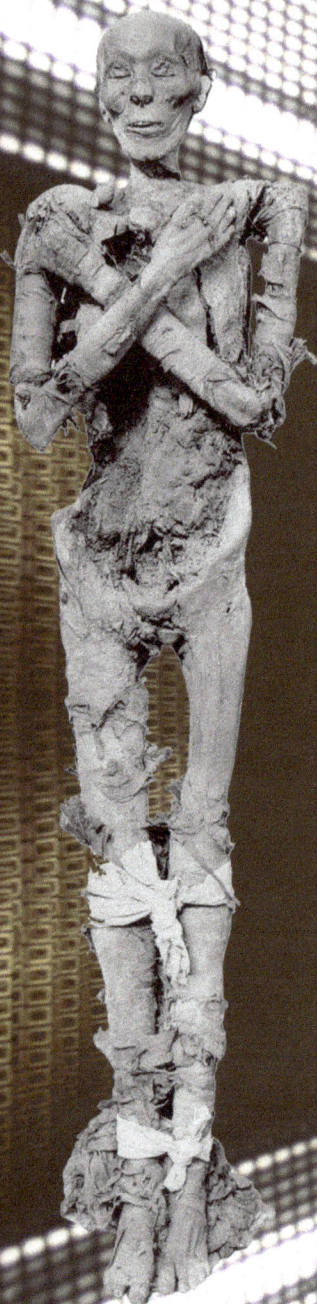

As we've already discussed, the objects that adorn our worlds (or don't) both express and create in a very real way the energy that surrounds us, and inevitably — whether we want them to or not — ultimately expresses us. And in that knowledge lies the very medicine-within-the-enema that releases the stuffed-up-elephant of my previous metaphor! While the family could have chosen any kind of artwork to hang there, despite their own apparently upbeat personalities, lining the endless hallways were extraordinarily expensive museum-worthy paintings of somber women with those creepy eyes-that-follow-you gazes, and every painting was a dark, heavy, watchful or strangely helpless vision of naked, victimized women sprawled on some ancient battlefield or lying tragically across some craggy rock. At the bottom of the spiraling stairs, the dark epicenter of the house was a yuck-soaked, nasty-ass, heartless place buried a floor below in the worst room I've ever set my foot in — a brooding, wood-paneled place ironically called the "entertainment room", though the kind of entertainment that had gone on through the years was easily felt and most likely still being played out in other dimensions as we examined its eerie-eyed,

Gargoyle-flanked fireplace and Satanic-feeling gothic adornments. As Cabby dealt with the Lunging Deads and the onslaught of questionable Neverborns and Lange sucked up and discarded emotions and energies the size of the Cosmos, while I begrudgingly punched it out with the Almighty Fuck-You-Asshole residue beyond that, it became exceedingly apparent that the awesome awfulness that had obviously been a part of the house since far before it was built was so thick and so tangible that no amount of sage, intent or command could possibly dis-create it. Having said that, if I'd known then what I know now, I would have taken every piece of evil-eyed portraiture, every gnarly-nasty-wooden, dragon-like, fireplace-flanking flourish, every bitterly-placed chunk of furniture that adorned that hell-vessel and chucked it all into a skip and given them the thumbs-up to take it away! And then! Muthafukkahs! Let's just see what you can cling onto then, eh!

But clinging-on is ultimately not what we are about, and no A-Bomb of energy needed to extricate the property's demons would have been worth getting in the way of our Happy Hour.

Interestingly enough, it was the kitchen — the smallest room in the giant mansion — that was the only refuge. A jolly, colorful place filled with copper pots and warm, wooden surfaces, the kitchen was the only agreed expression of the family's taste, and therefore devoid of the nasty vibes running rampant everywhere else. The daily, continual presence of all of the family members being there together created a much-needed energy island that allowed the most normal and congenial parts of themselves to breathe.

While our Ghost-Busting episode left the place peaceful for a few days, it was not long afterwards that the otherworldly grisliness picked up pace and intensity — and as far as I know remains there to this very day.

So if your kitchen is the only place that expresses you, and your dogs continue to fly through the air through the rest of the place, and you find yourself overwhelmed with an unhealthy attraction to dressing yourself up in Beef Jerky and the Pope pisses his pants upon entering your door, perhaps it's simply just time to move. That's certainly what us Slobs would do, and I highly recommend taking the easy road in these issues.

Mob Mentality simply aren't us, and so before we even start shifting and sucking and scraping and exfoliating, let's make sure we're in the right place for the right reasons, with a fridge that works and a basement full of beer instead of crazy-arsed-energy-sucking-nightmare-making Boogers!

POOP HAPPENS

You've been crapping since the day you were born, isn't it time you got used to it? You're a meat machine. We all are. We process foodstuffs, thoughts and all forms of energy. It's just a small part of what us meat puppets are born to do.

Madonna shits. The Pope shits. Branjelina shit, (although as far as I know, I believe they still do that separately). The Dalai Lama, the Queen, the next person you see, loads of people you don't even know, all of those uber-sexy girls in that band you love — every single person born on this planet, including Jesus has (hopefully) daily had to bend over and expel (usually with accompanying noises and smells) a completely transformed version of what entered at the other end of the body, earlier.

In fact, when you think of the entire human race squishing out at least, on average, one individual turd a day, that's a whole lotta poop going on!

Well, if you can't look your poop in the eye (sometimes it actually HAS an eye: in fact my cousin invited her now-husband to look at her poop cause it looked like a winking Pelican — she was so excited — he refused), then what you are *not* looking in the eye is your basic humanity, and the essential ebb and flow of energies that make all of us up.

It's a fact that people who are bunged up generally have trouble letting things go. Conversely, those who are constantly running for the shitter may have energy leakage they might want to examine and put in check. (Those who have lumps of corn in their turds, simply, have just eaten corn the night before).

As Above So Below is an unrestricted, all-embracing reality that does, indeed, extend to your inner environment — a whole other issue I'm just too lazy to cover here.

But, pulling up the point of poop: By not allowing your-self to positively embrace your own bodily functions, you are psychologically and energetically allowing yourself to skirt around some of the fundamental details of your world, which may or may not include those spackles on the underside of the bowl. (It's amazing how many people don't get down to the nitty-gritty of a good bowl clean!). And that skirting-around-the-issue-ness spirals upwards and outwards and all around you.

˙ I told you: This book is about paying attention to your surroundings — and that means all of it!

So what is it you've missed? — apart from delighting in that squinting Pelican you've just created?

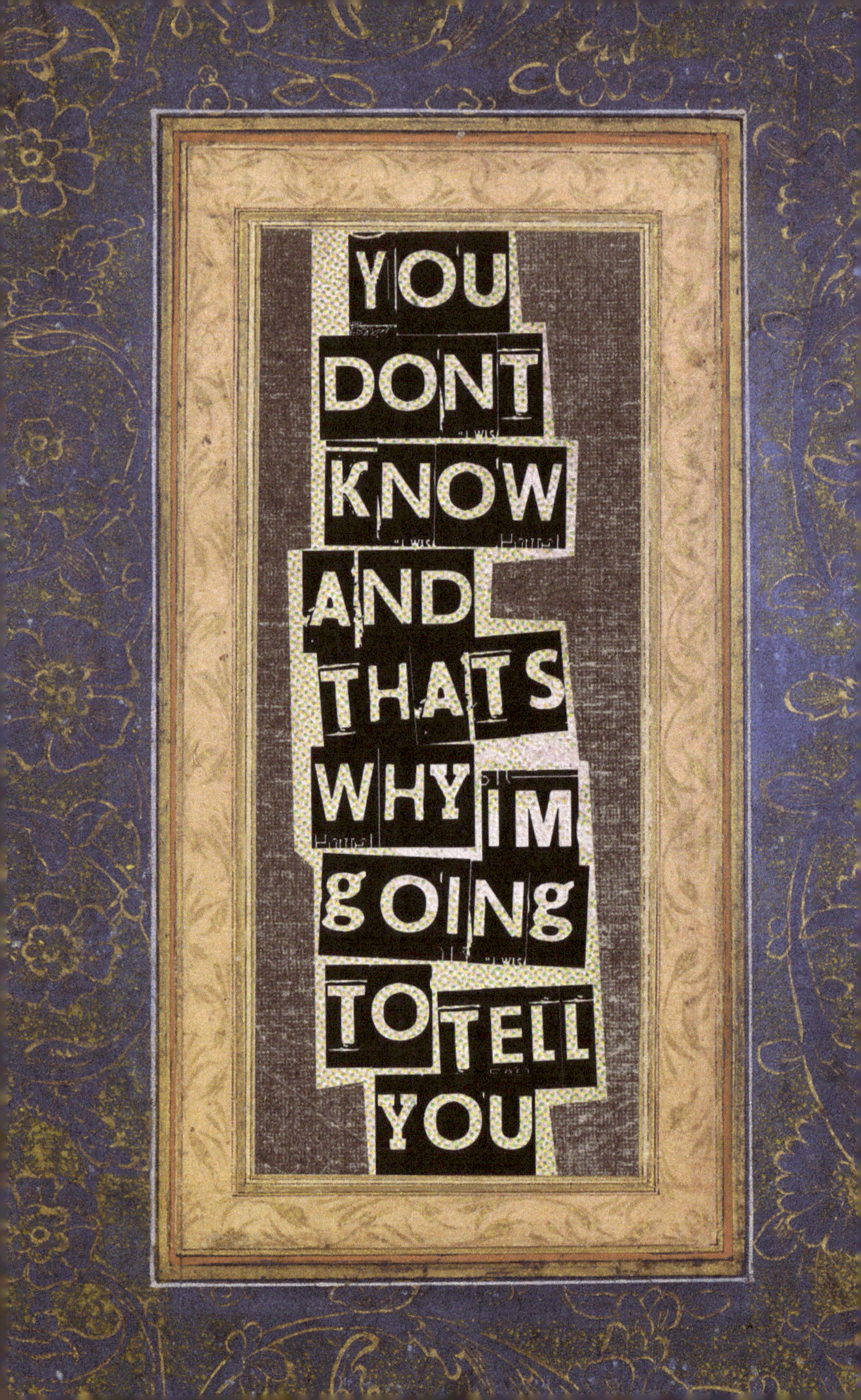
YOU
DONT
KNOW
AND
THATS
WHY IM
GOING
TO TELL
YOU

Awright, so you've walked in your front door, sent your mud-crusted shoes sliding into that skid-marked heap of underwear you've tossed into the hallway, chucked the keys in the designated rotting-fruit bowl, and, cracking open a cold one, slumped into your comfortable, soup-smeared armchair, and now you're ready to cast your critical eyes around your little kingdom.

It's all so familiar. Everything seems to be where it should be — well, maybe there are a few things here and there you could get around to sorting out, but it's kinda been, for ages, exactly as you wanted it — or, if not, at least you're used to it, so why change things just for the sake of changing?

You got your pictures up there on the wall (well, that's homey at least, isn't it), and even though you've never really been too fond of that one, it kinda hides that hole in the wall and the color is sort of ok, even though it's a portrait of dead pigeons strung up on a series of hooks in some medieval kitchen. Your partner gave you that creepy-eyed woman sketch (the frame is nice, though!), and you've never had the heart to tell him it kind of spooks you out, so that's gotta stay. And even though that sofa's a bit crammed into that corner, there's not a lot you can do with the space, so if you're gonna keep it — which you have to because you need it — well that's the only place it can be, and even though it means that every time you need to turn on the light you gotta spill yourself over it and sprawl in the dark, fumbling for the light switch, it's not that big a deal, 'cos you're used to it.

Apart from all of that, looking around, what is it that you're not seeing?

Sometimes, like the things I just mentioned, it's the stuff we've just grown used to. Sometimes it's the oh-so-obvious things — the elephants balancing their Bit Fat Arses right there on our heads — that escape our attention. Sometimes it's the stuff our senses have become so familiar with that only an outsider can draw our attention to it.

Last winter, filming a commercial in the driveway outside a home in the Midlands of England, the sun was going down and it was starting to get uncomfortably frosty.

The family who owned the place were a country-friendly bunch and, noticing us shivering, invited us inside for much-welcomed cups of hot tea. While we were more than happy to step out of the pending ice storm, stepping inside was like shoving our nostrils right up the rectum of an unwashed feline, and while the owners were obviously unaware of it, our outsiders' noses were tingling from the pungent smell of the legion of cats roaming about; our eyes itching from the fine hairs drifting through the air and clinging to every surface.

Though comfy-cozy to look at, our lovely hosts' home was obviously lacking vacuum bags and cleaning products — the heady, ingrained aroma of piss-soaked litter boxes causing us to abandon our hair-wrapped teacups and make a hasty back-track into the frosty but cat-less air outside.

So all in all, while we all have our zero-sight zones, I'm gonna make the assumption that you're not starting from the point of living in a joint crammed with ten-foot-high stacks of yellowing newspapers and discarded toilet rolls or a plateau of cat-feces rising up to your knees and a lifelong collection of butt-fluff stapled onto your walls (cause that shit's just kinda gross). But if you are, put the book down immediately and dial 99-UR-FUCKING-CRAZY and get back to me once the meds have kicked in. No worries, we all have time — until it runs out, of course.

For all of you others, sometimes it's good to start with a basic visual/olfactory check-list, scanning up, down and all around and using all of your senses like Daredevil (except he was blind, so that's not really the ideal example, although Daredevil is really neat in all kinds of uber-cool other-sensorial other ways) and honing in on how much better your utensil tray (and your life) might be without that vomit-like cack crusted like some ancient sediment beneath your gleaming silverware.

While I do believe that there are certain fundamentals (energetically speaking) rising from the grime-soaked, dusty, cobwebbed, cluttered, stark, haphazard, anal, ugly, pretty, grubby, sexy spaces of your world, any suggestions I am proposing are just that: suggestions. Run with them. Hold them in your hand and give 'em a good squeeze, like putty or a young recruit's testicles (why do they do that, anyway?) and see if they feel right. Or if you can hunt out other meanings to them.

Some things have a whole lotta meaning — part of the fun is recognizing the symbolism, which can often be hilariously literal or obvious and at other times deliciously cryptic. Other things are simply just crap-soaked clutter unnecessarily gunking up that wonderful matrix of energy that surrounds you. So, if something baffles you or if it's just a plain, annoying struggle trying to figure it out, forget trying to decipher every hieroglyph you've left yourself, and just shift or suck or dust or chuck the damn nuisance out. You'll feel the energy buzz around in its newly sparkled shape, or complete absence.

Alternatively, you can just switch off from the get-go, crank up your favorite play-list, and move and sweep and shapeshift your world and just stand back and see what happens!

CASE STUDY

WHAT GRIMES BENEATH

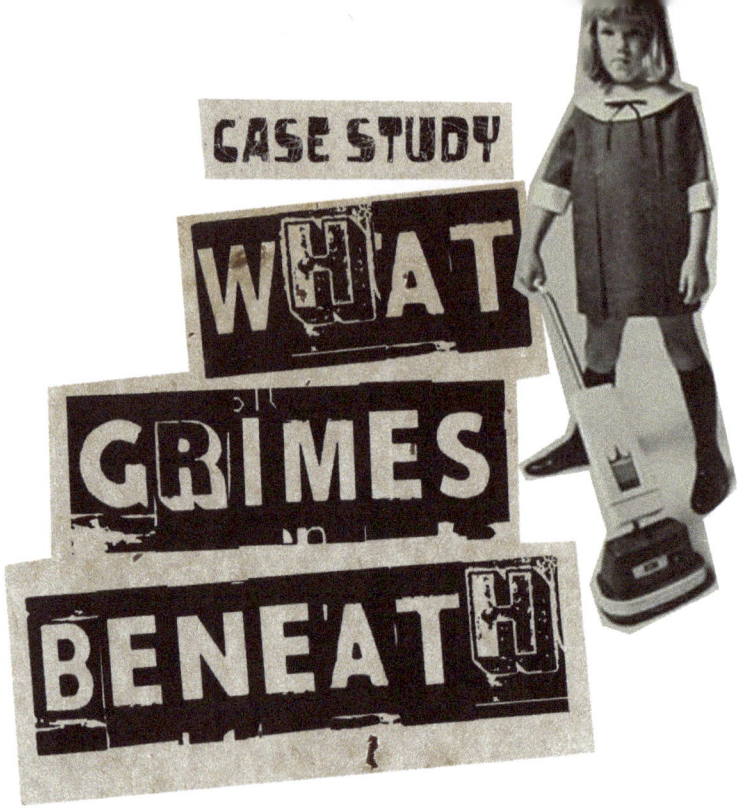

Sheba stood like a deer in the headlights of an oncoming truck, weeping uncontrollably as I continued to pull her entrails out, spilling them onto the floor.

Apart from the guts, wherever you looked around her sprawling, multi-leveled and rather gorgeous Georgian terraced house, not an object was out of place. Clean to the point of crazy-rigid, Sheba is that other kind of Virgo — that nitpicking, acid-tongued, know-it-all-yet-can't-see-the-woods-for-the-fuckin'-trees kind you all hear about (not the uber-grounded, well-rounded, omni-scopic brand like me) — who, for the sake of perfection, had so many rounds with plastic surgery that she was gazing at the world outta her nostrils. She was even known to bleach her coffee cup in between cups of coffee.

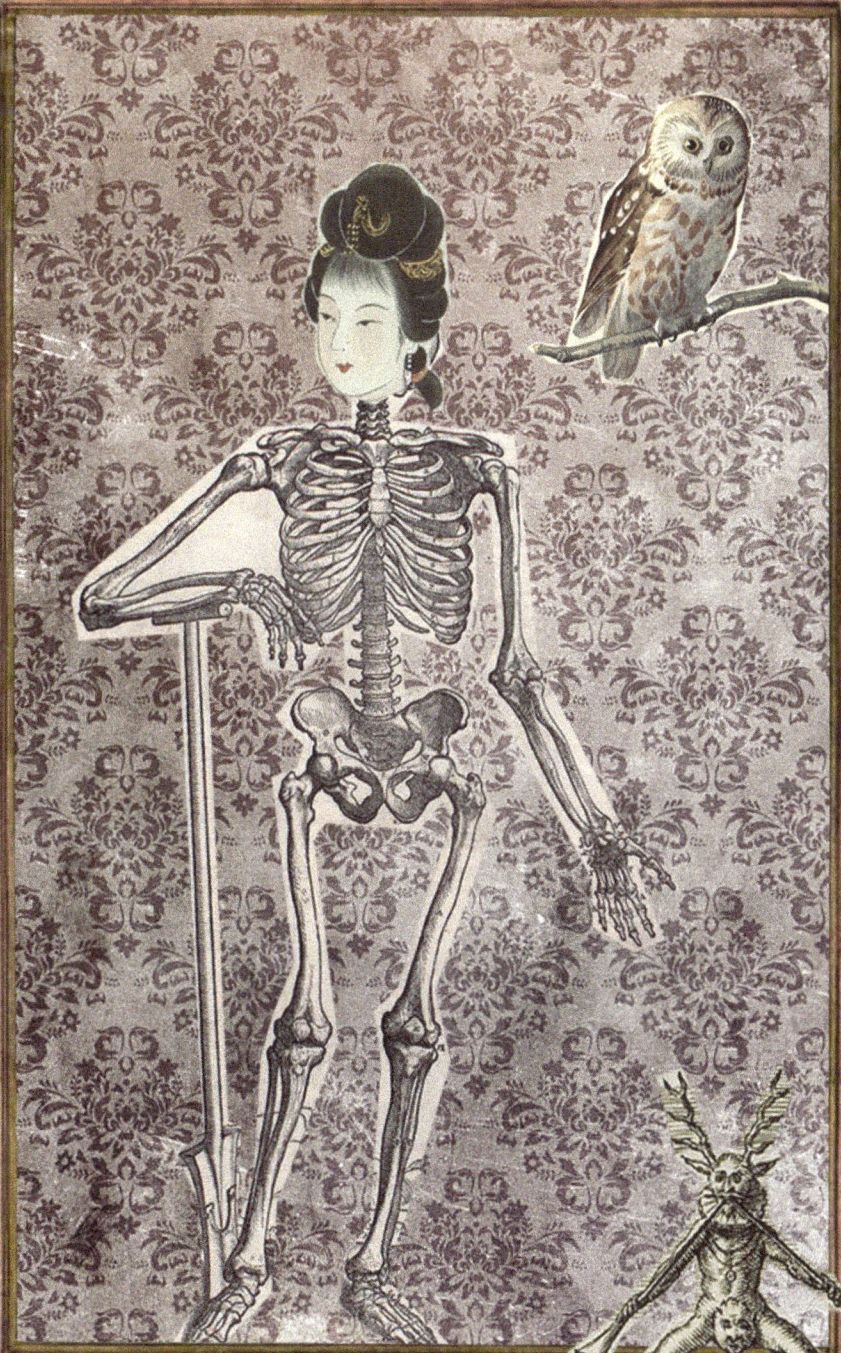

No object was allowed to linger — even when used — for longer than a few seconds before it was snatched up, thrown in its appropriate drawer, or placed with a snap! crackle! and pop! firmly into its designated holder or firmly planted into its never-to-be-fucked-with special spot.

The kitchen floor was washed at least three times a day, any tracks from outside vehemently eradicated, toilets scrubbed and re-scrubbed (you can never have a clean enough toilet!), family photos placed in an exact line, one behind the other with Sheba in front (which was the way, incidentally, the family itself was run!). The place was a virtual Temple dedicated to the Immaculate Gods of Cleaning Products.

But downstairs, What Lies Beneath The Surface was a very telling tattle-taler of what was really going on in Sheba's world.

Opening the door to it, you'd be excused for missing the fact that what you're peering into was not a closet, but actually the entranceway down to a rather large, long basement area. Coats and boots and carrier bags of all shapes and textures and sizes, books and poisons (yes, poisons!) greeted you just in case you didn't get the message that you were not supposed to be there! Tools and boxes of god-knows-what were all shoved into makeshift shelves and dangling on hooks and hanging on hangers and tacked on every surface.

The symbolism was neon-sign high. Here, hidden in the depths, were the things about Sheba — beyond all the shining, bleached surfaces and neat placing of objects, beyond the Designer's decorative touches and the cushions you weren't supposed to settle back into — that she did not want to surface, the things that were meant to remain unseen.

Risking strangulation by the myriad arms of The Coats Of Seasons Past, entangling themselves around your throat as you navigated the treacherous few feet towards a set of steep, creaky stairs, only the brave (such as me) or the oblivious (such as Sheba) would have the nerve to descend the shifting planks that threatened at every step to flip like Tiddly Winks and topple you arse-over-tea-kettle into the murky, must-soaked underbelly of the happy-looking Homes & Gardens upper world.

Like the thorny forest of some Grimm's Fairy Tale, below-stairs was — as well as the storage area for the Unwanted and the Never-To-Be-Discarded — curiously enough, the working laundry room: a washer and drier precariously stacked on top of one another and shoved into the back recesses of the dungeon, so that the daily task of washing and drying also included a tour of the guts and psyche of the Queen of Clean.

While the rest of the basement was a horrific-smelling, dust and mildew-covered disaster, the cleaning area was an even more weirdly, shockingly rancid affair. The carpet at the base of the machine, where the laundry would be thrown prior to being shoved into the washer, was grey with pungent-smelling mould and soggy, caked-in spillages of a decade's worth of washing-up powders. The surfaces of the machines themselves were almost comically coated with mounds of festering, discolored liquids and powders, piled and dripping like century's-old heaps of pigeon poop.

Like entering a cave filled with stinking bat-guana, this bacteria-infested underworld, with its lack of light and boxed-up jumble of unwanted things, kind of (well, exactly) mirrored what was going on with Sheba, both in her family and her health.

No wonder that she'd been through three different chemo and radiation therapies for a recurring cancer (she's a fighter, that one, and has it beat!) or that the family, like the unwanted issues at the bottom of the house, were shoved into their private worlds: the teenage daughter locking herself in a room that Sheba refused to clean and therefore had self-styled itself into the "fuck you" attitude of its inhabitant and looked more like a crack-ho's toilet than a bedroom; the young son similarly hiding underneath a mound of chocolate bars and junk food in front of his Game Boy in his own room; the husband, with his requisite bottle(s) of wine, slumped in the living room watching an endless loop of racing programs; and Sheba herself, smoking in the back garden, door closed, unaware that her Normal was well advanced into most other people's Totally Crazy.

My offer of cleaning the basement was something I soon regretted, for every removed object just seemed to reveal a never-ending Mary Poppins bag of goods: pianos and refrigerators hidden beneath stacks of clothing, suitcases, tools, products of all kinds, toys and lamps and dishes and paintings and plumbing kits and self-help kits (never opened) and unrecognizable-by-virtue-of-grime things...

While at first my determination to tackle this whirlwind of objects was appealing to Sheba, it wasn't long before the energetic significance of those hidden voices came screaming at us in full force.

The raw emotions from all that junk coming out of their hiding places into the light of day sent her bawling and shaking and unravelling before my gunge-stung eyes.

The effect was so extreme that in the end — both to pacify her and to abort what seemed as if it would need at least another reincarnation to tackle — the objects yanked out went back into their cave.

Sheba stopped trembling and went back out into the yard to have a calming smoke.

And, not long after that, the family split, the house was sold, and Sheba was back in the hospital.

Such extreme examples of rampant stagnation can, in fact, create an energetic blast — usually uplifting. But in the case of Sheba, a person who preferred to keep a facade going and even endure the cancer resulting from the stress of keeping that hatch closed, the release of energy can be a little overwhelming, to say the least.

By doing things at your own pace, and having fun doing so, the energy shifting will align itself naturally. In this case I learned a valuable lesson about not helping others, because the pace at which I was eliminating and exposing was clearly too much for Sheba, who, in reality, would rather have continued with the cluttered disgustingness below the stairs — and did.

Doing this kind of energetic shuffle for yourself should be fun and personal. Like an excellent and much-needed spiritual whack-off, you gauge the bits that feel good, back off from those that don't, and get that fabulous energetic sploosh! that's all in your own time, on your own terms and leaves you feeling absolutely rockin'!

At least that's what it feels like to me.

BACK IN THE CLOSET

I'm not exactly a clothes-horse, mainly because pretty much the second most aggravating experience I can imagine (the first being sticking pins into my eyeballs — something I've never done but can imagine would be pretty annoying) is queuing up for the privilege of being crammed into some tight little cubicle to try on items that don't fit or suit you, only to emerge again, sweaty and sticky and irritated, still in your tatty t-shirt and the only jeans you like to wear anyway and no closer to looking like one of those washboard-stomached guy-models who'd look terrific wearing a sack full of boogers anyway.

Despite this, in that mysterious manner in which the Universe appears to operate, my closet seems to be set to automatic self-stock, and every year I find it necessary to pull out bags and bags of clothing I never knew I had and certainly can't remember ever buying — and definitely have never worn.

And then there are those treasured items you *did* wear once upon a time, a long time ago when dinosaurs ruled the earth and shoulder pads seemed perfectly acceptable even for us men, which you keep just in case shoulder pads come back in style again, ignoring the voice screaming at you that you'd look fuckin' ridiculous in them, just as you did twenty years ago. And of course, afterwards, you went through that baggy urban thang, which allowed you to totally binge on beer and potato chips until you realized you looked less urban and more like one of those fat Middle-Americans screaming at one another on some icky loser talk show. But now you've gone kinda minimalist with jeans and t-shirts and still keep that other stuff on standby just in case, along with a bunch of hideous ties that one day might just have an occasion weirdly designed for them, and a bunch of broken belts you're never gonna get around to fixing, and not-quite-white-anymore underwear that've lost their elastic. And then there's the kinky leather phase carefully hidden in the back as if your mother is gonna fly out from Canada and surprise you by springing out at you from her hiding place in your closet, and even though you don't do that kinda stuff anymore and kinda never did, cows have died for that shit to be created, which is why there's that extra ten pairs of shoes you'll never wear again, crammed into a rickety, annoying wooden stack of shoe shelves that never did what they were supposed to do, but you put them in your closet in an organizational fit and there they've remained, hovering above you on the top shelf, threatening to tumble down and brain you every time you open the door.

My friend Lunar, a bi-polar Gemini (like the world needs one of those), who insisted on having his socks "tossed like a salad" and thrown into a basket all mixed up so you'd have to search for the matching pairs, went ape-shit like a hornet on crack when I paired them up. Which says a lot about how someone's psychotic inner dialogue and general ungrounded-ness can express itself even in the foot sections of your closet.

Needless to say, like everywhere else in your world, your closet has a few things to say about who you are, and some of those things should be culled like unwanted relatives and banished to your local charity shop.

HEART YOU!

It's important to stress at this stage that not everything is about filth and grime. Sometimes it's just about stuff. Too much stuff — or sometimes, as we saw in the case of Butch, too little — or the wrong stuff. Or the right stuff but put together in a way that's like a tiny little muffled flare from our psyche into the Universal web, hoping to be seen.

And this is where, Slob, you start seeing (again) how you and Creator (or Buddha, or Pixie Boo-Boo, or as I like to call him, Gregg Cihangir Masuak) are the same thing, kinda like best pals slipping notes to one another back and forth in the classroom, adding to them and giggling until neither of you/me/he/she/it knows any longer who wrote what first and to whom.

It's all signs and signals, reminders and taps on the shoulders, this duck-and-dive between objects, identity and Spirit, and it doesn't matter a damn what angle you look at it from, which makes it completely blameless and captivating and fun! Make no mistake: there's no end to this shit. You are always passing those notes between you/ourselves, you delightful little spiritual scallywags!

And with that in mind, you can relax and enjoy the process, 'cos sure as the grease gets scraped outta the garbage disposal, there'll be another fresh new piece of cack somewhere else — and that's just frikkin' dandy!

One example of how you-talk-to-yourself-creator-talks-to-you-as-you-both-talk-to-each-other-yadda-yadda can be witnessed in the kind of thing you'd never normally pick up on (except now you got this book, and you're reading it, and you're not seeing your life through the eyes of a Slob any more, but through the lense of a newly gifted Spiritual Slob) is case-in-point Deniz, a lovely Turkish friend of mine with the deepest brown eyes and the kind of complexion you'd imagine some mermaid might have — pale and flawless like tiny little fish have been nibbling and exfoliating her constantly like those little vats of fish you see in Balinese foot spas — which is totally appropriate as her name means "the sea".

I'm always envious when someone's name means some-thing — anything — and especially when it means some-thing cool, like the guy I mentioned earlier who designed and illustrated this book, Emir, whose name means "Prince" and "Power" or some shit like that, while my name, Gregg, just means Gregg, or perhaps the sound you make when you're choking on your tongue.

Which is why I added the name Cihangir, 'cos I fuckin' love it, and it means "World Conqueror" and that's where I'm at, babies! (Though I see myself more as a Benevolent Conqueror of Hearts and Minds and Souls and stuff, not the kind of stupid conqueror that cuts off people's heads and moronic shit like that.)

Anyhow, mermaid-esque Deniz's love life has been in the shitter for so long she can't even remember the last time she had need for a personal lubricant — and no matter what you say that shit's important, 'cos your energy centers are like big old chain stores in a giant shopping mall, and when one shuts down it leaves the mall feeling kinda tatty. And once that mall starts feeling tatty, there's less people shoppin' around, and before you know it you got a fine but completely abandoned mall with a few bubble gum machines and a Gymboree but little else, and that energy kinda sucks.

You gotta keep all your chain stores buzzing, all of them — but then again, that's probably just my Scorpio Rising talking, and us Scorpionics are pretty much just a bunch of boners with heads like periscopes searching out the next available orifice.

Back to Deniz, now vehemently single. And let me now quickly scramble to the podium, tap the mic, and announce, before you shout at me: NOT ALL OF US HAVE TO BE IN A RELATIONSHIP!

I get it, I get it, I get it. However, in this case, vehement single-dom was — even though she protested was her conscious choice — in fact the result of a batch of uber-shitty affairs with some extremely poorly chosen dudes (or did the Cosmos choose them for a rather yucky little learning curve, I don't know). Which, rather than leaving her spinning in the delicious, dizzy dance that love can bring, had left her punch-drunk noggin' whirling like an old rattly kid's toy, all jittery and smashing into the walls and wearing her down till she just didn't want to frikkin' spin anymore.

Apart from the fact that she's my pal, I couldn't help but feel for sweet Fuck-You-Love Deniz, because you could just sense the longing in her soul, kinda like the sickly-sour poopy-smell of a pulp mill when the wind shifts from north to east and you're standing in the back yard with your steaks sizzling on the barbeque and your nostrils suddenly get all confused and stacked up with an uncomfortable mixed-bag of disparate olfactory cross-references for a moment.

You couldn't help but notice how little things just spilled out from her being into her sweet little environment — little things that to us Spiritual Slobs now, after traveling this journey as we have (notice you're no longer stomping and stamping and angrily cracking open that beer and turning the TV set on!) recognize as energy spurts seeding themselves into our reality so that we can recognize ourselves in them.

In the homey environment that Deniz had chosen to manifest, almost all the photographs she had on the mantelpiece were single shots of her.

"No shit, Sherlock," you sneer. (Oops! there's that attitude again!) "Not exactly earth-shattering news when you're several years down the line from your last shag and determinedly partner-less!"

But what was telling was that deliciously tiny little "look at me" item that you Spiritual Slobs are coming to recognize more and more within your own environments. Isolated on one shelf was a framed photograph of herself, alone — but like *really* alone — which was weird, because she was seated, a distant figure, smiling sweetly like a kid posing in front of some toy she wanted but hadn't the nerve to ask for, in front of the frikkin' Taj Mahal. No other person in sight!

Now for those of you in the know — and now for those of you who aren't — the Taj Mahal is perhaps one of the world's most significant homages to love from an emperor to his (dead) wife. Its presence literally reeks of love, of yearning, made even more poignant by the fact that it was an apparently perfect and now, by virtue of wifey's demise, Endless Love (just like that film with Brooke Shields and some guy named Martin Hewitt who apparently now sells home inspection merchandise).

Directly behind that strangely shy and oh-so-very-lonely photograph — that very personal tribute to lonesome individuality against a backdrop of undying love — and shoved into the shadows of the shelf was a personal diary with a three- dimensional heart on its cover. And nothing but blank pages inside it!

Despite Deniz' protestations of fidelity to herself and herself alone — always the one to (almost angrily) slam you if you suggested that there just might be someone out there for her (whether she wanted them or not) — Deniz, or Taj Mahal-as-Deniz, positioned, just for herself, a clue as to the energetic reality she *really* lived in, going so far as to place a book within easy reach of her own self, ripe and ready for her vision of love to be rewritten according to her own desires: not the scary twirling goo-goo-go-round of the past, but a Mahal-ian temple of commitment and truth.

Such silent yoo-hoos from our souls are not haphazard pieces of brick-a-brack stacked randomly or accidentally, but the karaoke bar of the Universe screaming for us to turn up the volume, grab the mic and belt out our favorite song — which of course, we now are!

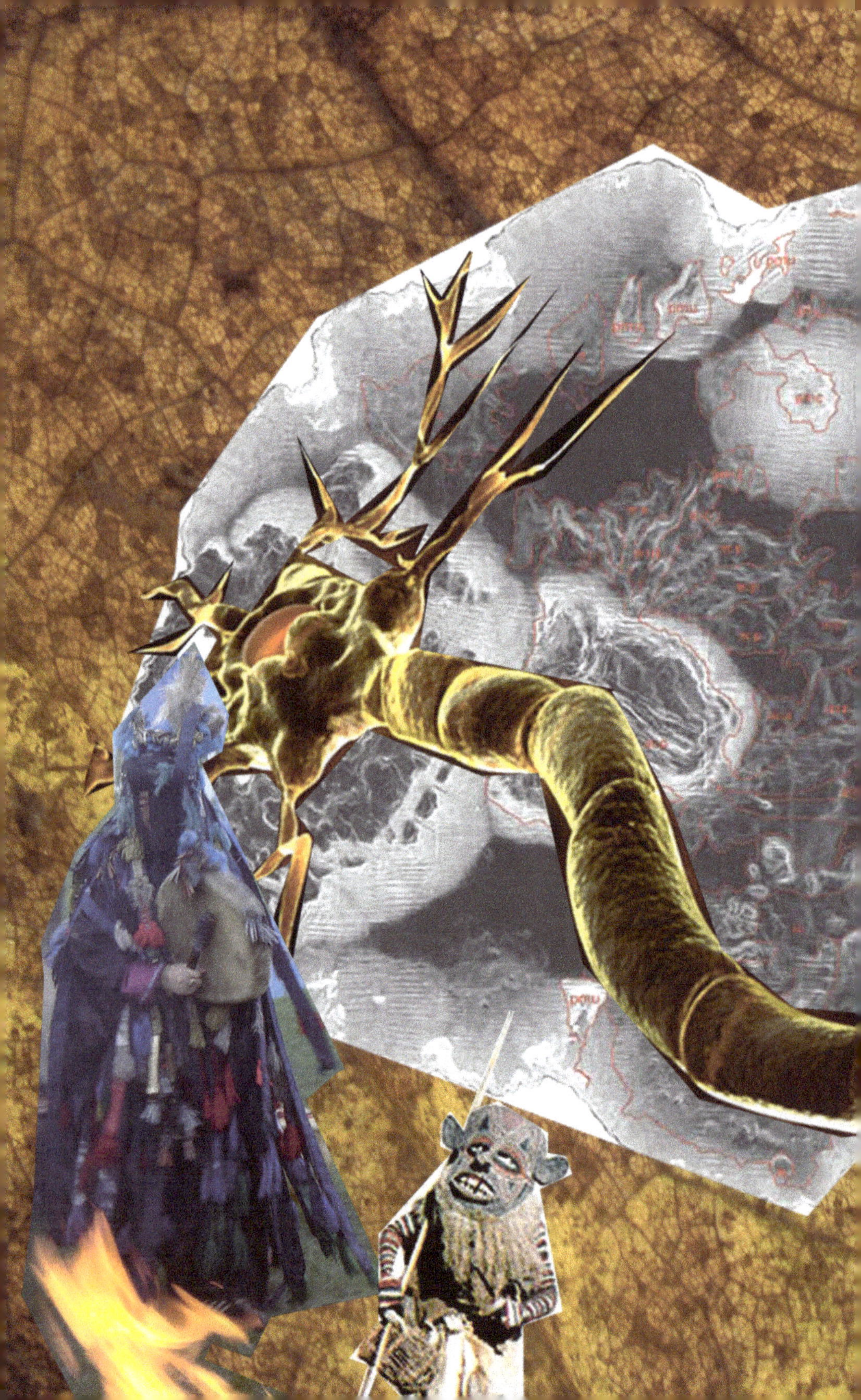

NOW A CONTRADICTION!

IT'S ONLY CACK!

Wading through knee-high rivers of puke is certainly no longer an option for the Spiritual Slob, now that we realize it's not just puke any longer but the upchuck of our very energetic beings. But we are, after all, still Slobs, and with the additional knowledge that no amount of cleaning, shifting, altering or eliminating will ever create a Perfect World (as we've not signed up for Perfect World-ness on this particular planet) plus the fact that this is all supposed to be interesting and (yes, again!) FUN, it's important that we approach things with a light-hearted touch and not with broom-up-your-arse rigidity or freaked-out undercurrents as another molecule of dust settles onto your freshly polished surfaces.

So if you're frantically and angrily scraping the shit off your shoes (having had many happy pooches in my time, I know how hard it is to scrape the shit off your shoes without being frantic or angry) or cussing as you pull the weeds out from the footpath leading to your front door, then you're creating the very garbage you're meant to be uncreating.

Which is why, as I mentioned earlier, the furious frenzy of uber-intented Feng Shui or panic-stricken Affirmations just do not work. There's a fine line between easy-going expecting-without-expecting-the-best intention and the willful force-feeding of intent into the hungry craw of the Universe.

In fact, there's a well-known example (well, I know it at least!) about a guy whose career was less than terrific, who with great effort and not just a small feeling of panic went out and bought a bucket of red paint, slapping it against the walls with the tense hope that this, at last, would save his career from dipping down into the crapper (actually, it was his bathroom he was painting, even more appropriate to the tale!) and creating, with every splash of sticky toxic liquid, an anguished tale of doom and failure with the expectation that unless the room was red — and red immediately — his life was going to spiral down into the pits.

So, Slobs, what do you think happened? It didn't help that his least favorite color was, in fact, red — which was quickly painted a neutral color once the new tenants moved in after the house was returned to the bank and our hero became a Barista at Starbucks. (Actually, I have no idea what happened to the guy, but I'm sure he's decided that, Feng Shui or not, Career Corner or not, red is just not the color for him.)

So, just as the Creator (or Lakshmi, or Zeus or the All-Stillness-Of-Everything) just hangs back and lets us do all the work, we too, being precisely that entity in our tight, sexy little slabs of meat and bone and fat are more likely to create happy tales than sob stories if our intentions remain true.

There's no kidding ourselves about how we *feel* about stuff. So if you've located the voices in your apartment that are shouting: "Look at this! No wonder you're such a fat ugly loser!" then it's best to switch on your favorite tune-device to top volume, slam on "Walking On Sunshine" or some similarly happy, dopey song, and deal with the junk without thinking about it, knowing — as you will soon come to know in your heart of hearts — that, being the Deity Him/Her/Itself, you don't really have to think too much about what you are doing. Just keep the expectation and judgment on the sidelines and walk on that sunshine!

CRYSTALS & CRAP

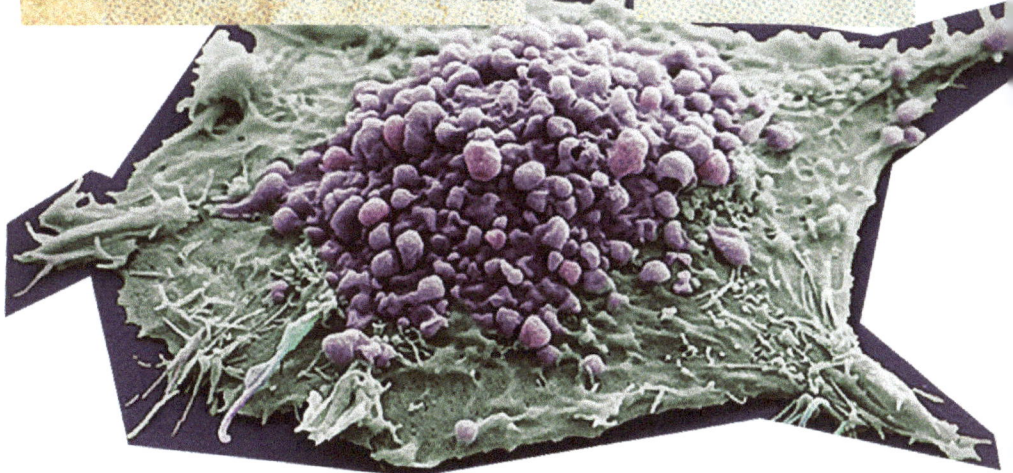

And, while we are on the subject of you-as-your-home (which, in case you missed it, is kinda the subject of this whole book) and Feng Shui and energy and shit, no number of Dreamcatchers or Crystals hung or Baguas of different colors sticky-taped in your Prosperity Corner or Weird Fish you hate — stuffed like ugly, gliding, mouth-gaping-open turds in your aquarium — or little Angel Statues bought on QVC or Rocks of every size and shape and color and energetic composition are gonna do jack-motherfuckin'-shit unless they're there because you damn well love them and have placed them wherever they are with a light-hearted intent, rather than a I-gotta-do-this-now-or-my-life-is-going-to-hell attitude.

My best friend, when we were living together, would take the firings of my spiritual furnace — those things I vehemently believed in — find the things he liked, and apply them in that sickeningly arty-beauty-ga-ga Libran way, with just the perfect balance of "I believe" and "I'm not really convinced" — in particular becoming fired up by the sheer awesomeness of dazzlingly expensive crystals, placed with additional expense around the place by a much-heralded Crystal Expert whose own place was a crowded apartment so jam-packed with stones that the impact was more crazy-obsessed than just sheer let's-give-it-a-whirl beauty.

The pragmatic Libran that he was/is, Alphonse would fork out the dough, choosing the stones that moved his soul and let the "expert" place them before sneaking them into zones he preferred once she left — most likely steered to do so by virtue of his Higher-Other-Knowledge — simply letting them be with no further thought on the matter other than sheerly loving those craggy, rocky, light-spinning creations of gorgeousness.

Meanwhile I, in my recently acquired Feng Shui frenzy, had Bagua'd every object in the place, shifted and pulled bits and pieces of crap into the appropriate energetic corners, bought hideous factory-made objects from Chinatown without thinking that just perhaps the antithesis of prosperity is an ugly cluster of plastic coins hanging from every corner or cheap resin frogs shoved by the door. Even the arty-cool devices of my own creation were slung up like desperate posters in the face of the Universe, screaming out: PLEASE HELP ME, I'M-A GOIN' DOWN!

Needless to say (and I do concur that there might be just simple personal fate at play here), the lighter touch with the heavier lay-out of cash and true appreciation on Alphonse's part seemed to act like an unstoppable slipstream that pulled Alphonse to greater and greater heights, security and joy, while my heavy-handed sticking-to-the-rules acquisition of what was truly and simply ugly junk created just that: desperate, ugly junk in my life.

Which is not to say I advocate forking out a lotta dough just to get you in the cosmic slipstream. Attitude, remember? It's all about the attitude!

Meanwhile, it doesn't take much of a rocket scientist to figure out that the zillions of Chinese slinging all this shit up everywhere are not all billionaires and that, unless you really really think they are uber-groovy to look at, energetically speaking, a pukey bunch of synthetic flowers can not possibly have the same delicious fairy dust as the real thing, and yes I do believe that the Almighty Whatever did create things that can be ripped out of the earth and shoved in a vase in order to make your home look super sweet.

Of course it's up to you if you want the real thing or the reflection of ugly cheap stuff. (We are what we eat, so to speak.)

Another friend of mine was so desperate for a Life-Changing Koi Pond by her front door that the battle for Good-Energy-At-The-Entrance-To-Her-Home became so embittered it caused a rift in her marriage, and the whole thing fell apart after a couple years of squabbling for the right Feng Shui set-piece. Which of course probably meant that they really weren't on the same plane in the first place, but also ironically and pointedly illustrates how trying to push the river can still simply end up with you falling over the waterfall.

And the crazy crystal-stuffed-apartment-dwelling Expert? She was crushed by a massive Weights Machine at the gym. I kid you not. Which was, perhaps, a rather painful joke by the Universe telling her to lighten her load.

SKID MARKS

The heart of every home can be the living room, kitchen or, in Bismarck's case, the upstairs toilet. Literally, whatever is most central in where you live is also most central to your inner Universe, like the hub of a wheel that — depending on whether it's gleaming and sparkly like the   brilliant star that you are or languoring in fetid belchy-ness like Jabba The Hutt keeping your Inner Princess Leia (and c'mon, you-know-you-wanna-Leia!) from busting free — can determine the tone of what, precisely, is spinning around you.

So as Bismarck's life was in the dumps, it was no surprise that where he *took* a dump — the one and only bathroom in the house shared by both he and his flat-mate — was like one awful communal skid mark: a grungy pube-spattered mini-vista of the lethargy in which he found himself putrefying.

Like the stoners they were, the little microcosm reflected the jumbled confusion and haphazard mutual energies in which they coalesced. Fingernail clippings cohabited with stacks of smeared, grimy makeup; twists of used dental floss comingled with rusty razors and new ones; coagulated toothpaste and talcum powder and shaving cream and ointments and oil-smeared containers and graying soap dishes. It was all just a giant coagulated, stuck Yuk.

Now before you scream at me (again), I leap energetically onto the podium once more and say that, while I remain non-judgmental about your particular lifestyle and choices and shit, and understand that spliffing up every morning might be one of those choices, no "recreational" drug has ever (except in the mind of the user) made him or her prettier, smarter, funnier or genuinely focused. And that's a fact, and you know I'm telling the truth because by now you've come to realize you're not talking to some stick-in-the-mud Capricorn or pushy-pants, unthinking, slam-your-opinion-against-the-wall-anyway Aries, but a grounded, focused Virgo who happens to know everything about everything, and that's a fact too! I have yet to see any home whose heart is anything else than an expression of the brilliant or cluttery, stale or spirited, sterile or loving mental, physical, emotional and spiritual state of its inhabitants. So, apart from the entrance to your place — which can indicate just what comes knocking (or not) at your door — the best place to start, as with all things, is at the heart.

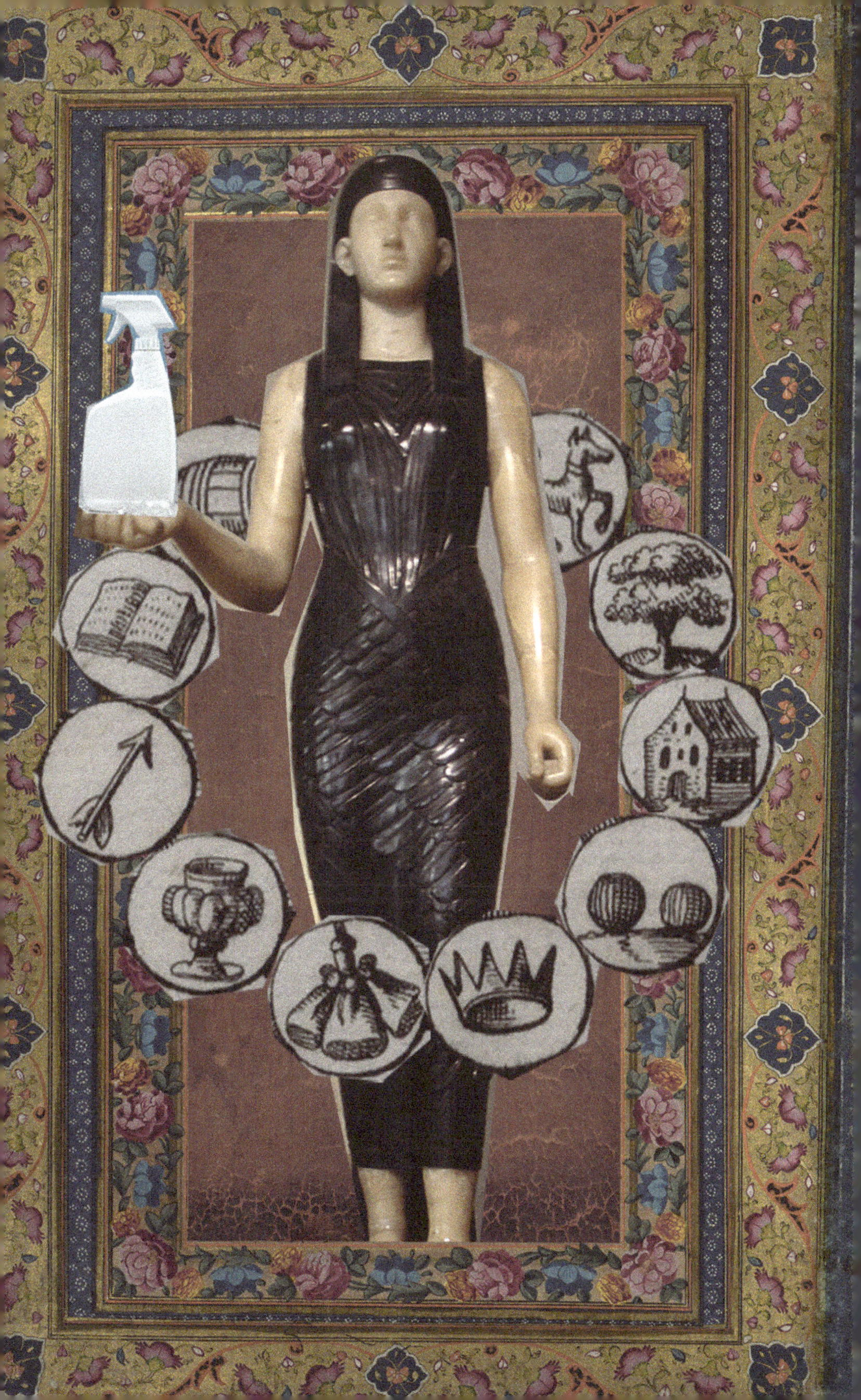

Even us wise-ass spiritual know-it-alls need to triple-check what we're spilling out into our worlds, despite our often snotty vehemence about having our shit together in that department.

Those Vision Boards — so often touted as sure-fire Super-Highways to the building and achieving of your dreams — are often assembled with an undertone of whining and pining and the angst of not having the very things being pinned up on them, so that they lose the very fun of what they're supposed to be doing in the first place.

And then they sit there, month after month, year after year, reminding us of the things we still don't have, creating an energetic Ouch! as we walk past.

I went to one house with a Vision Board that was a telling mess, falling askew from its hook at a precarious angle, its pinned-up images tattered and barely visible, the board itself cracked and smashed against the wall, half-hidden by stacks of unopened mail and magazines and dirty coffee mugs and empty take-away packages, so that its real intent seemed to be a determination to block the very dream it was meant to represent.

Like a final middle-finger to this vaguely funny but mainly sad personal bit of dream-bashing, nearby, oddly discarded in the centre of the room, was a big old chicken bone. And I mean *old*.

Now what would you think about leaving something rotten and picked clean of its sustenance right there in the centre of your world with your dreams smashed and buried in the corner, eh?

Sometimes the signals we leave for ourselves are like giant road-wrecks we don't even notice, even as we blindly step over the carnage and the hissing red flares in order to get to where we think we want to go.

Remember this: The collage doesn't stop at the boundary-edges of that Vision Board, pals. Your whole life is a Vision to be nurtured and shined-up, with a lightness of touch, a sense of fun, and a dash of easy expectation. So slap that noggin' of yours a few times before you start looking. Sharpen up. And see what funny little notes you've staple-gunned onto your own heart!

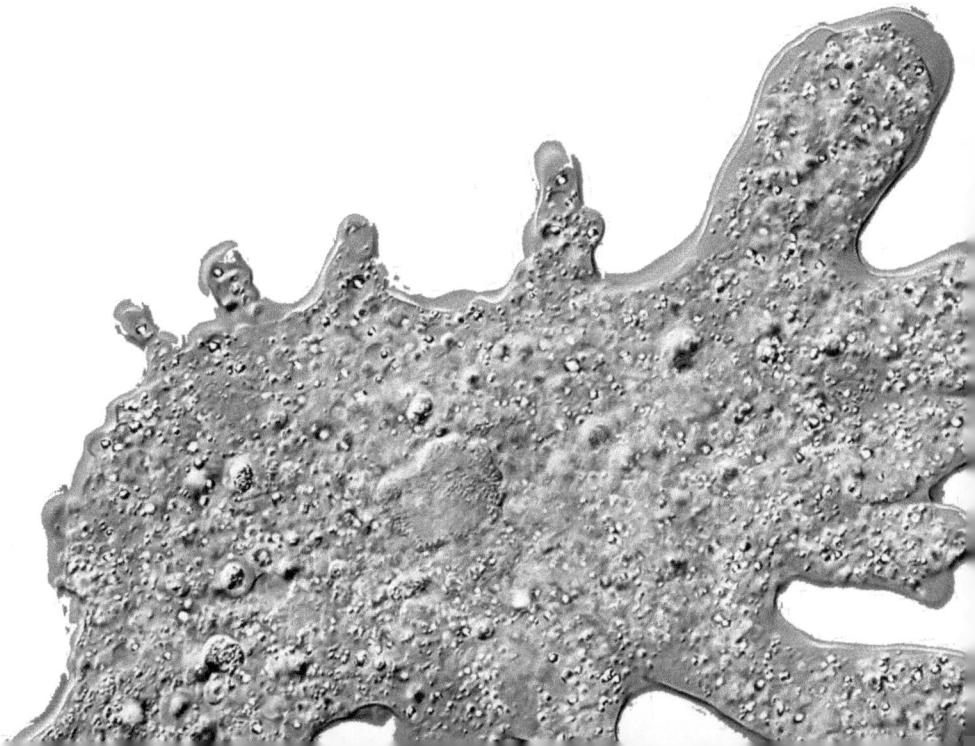

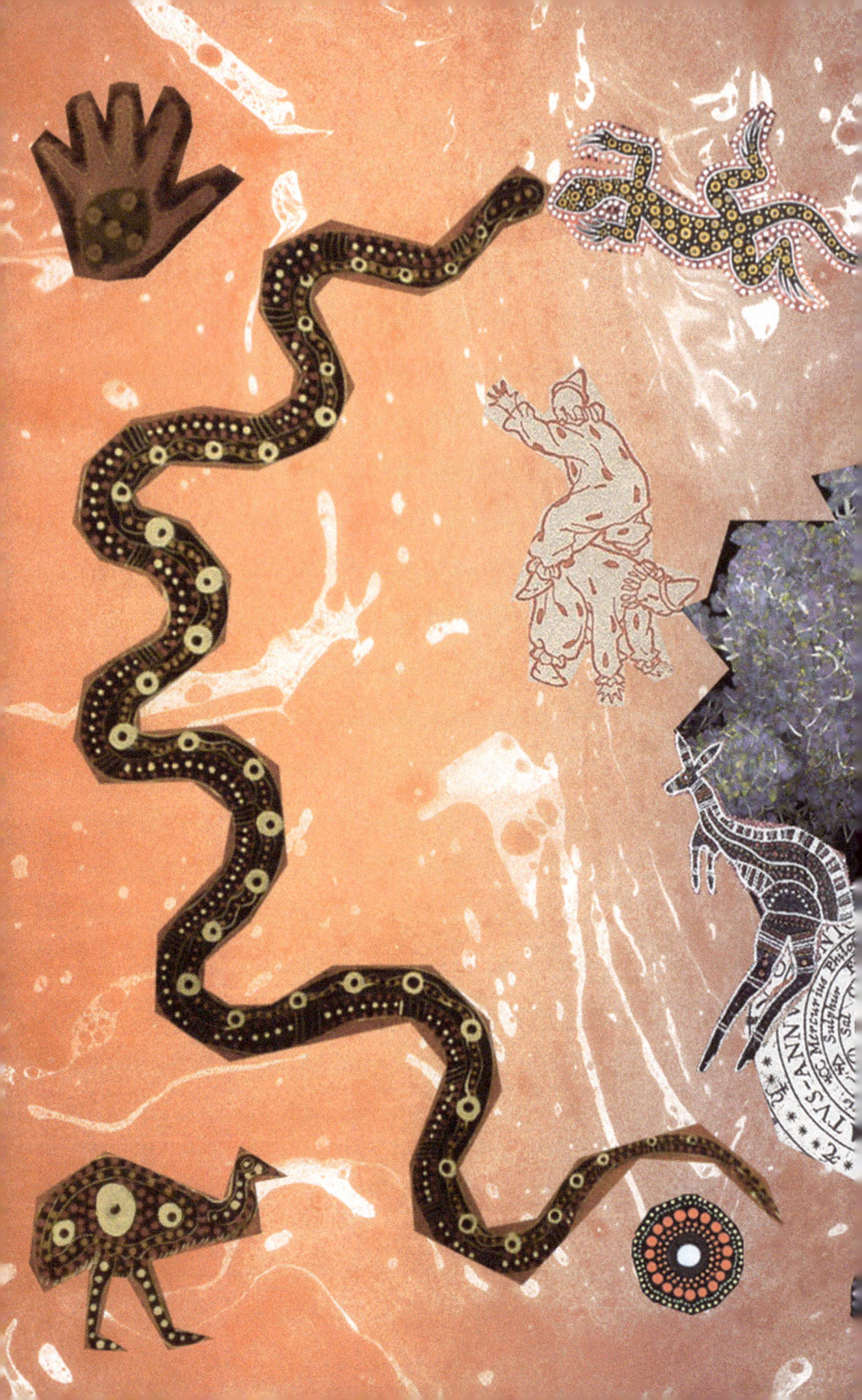

CRITTERS YOU WANT.... ....AND CRITTERS YOU DON'T

Animals are great energy shifters, and that I do know for a fact (along with everything else), having cared for just about every animal in the whole animal kingdom all at the same time for many years. (It did get kinda mental after a while, especially with the parrots, who had a penchant for ear-splitting screams during business calls, making me sound like some creepy thug who'd tied up a couple of panicking old ladies and just suddenly had the urge to set up a job interview!)

With all their bouncing pouncing squawking whistling twittering screeching and (underneath the watery surface) glug glug glugging, the beasts you choose to bring into your world are not only great at kicking the crap outta stale energy, but, being earth-attached, they are experts at sucking bad energy out of you too. In which case be aware, cause they do this shit without a judgmental moment, and personally I know what's gone on in some homes during breakups, and stressful events like that can end up creating some pretty bad stuff in the beasts and birds, only because they're happy to take the pressure off you when and if they can.

So make sure you love 'em up, even when they poop outside their cages, cack up bits of grass on the kitchen floor, or start humping the legs of the dinner guests.

Meanwhile, while many animals are super-aware cosmic bridge-gaps evolving (I believe) towards our Advanced Human Slobbishness (my friends' dog Emma is, I believe, a highly intelligent human being dressed up in a big wooly suit that makes her look like a giant Sasquatch), they are not aware of (or don't care about) the stuff that flies off, scatters around, or comes out of them. Well actually that's not entirely true, but that's a whole other Universe to explore, like a dolphin's stare. But for practical purposes, since dogs can't handle dust pans (well Emma might be able to, but she's keeping that up her wooly sleeve for the time being), it's up to us humans to not only take care of the obvious, but also the miniscule stuff that makes people sneeze the tea out of their nostrils when they plump down on that microbe and dander soup you call a sofa.

On that note, did you realize that inside the average pillow after about three months there's about two hundred bazillion jillion mites, with their accompanying bazillion jillion mite shites, all adding up to about one-third of your pillow's weight? Gross!

Before you start smashing my face against the laptop, Mister or Miss Smarty-Google-Wiki-Pants, I concede that I might have gotten a couple of those figures wrong (I pre-warned you about my being a Slob, and that goes for figures too), but you get the gist. Give or take a jillion, and that's a whole lot of extra yuk! you just don't need to be dreaming on!

What kind of nocturnal energy those little bastards are sending out to you in your sleep is anyone's guess, but it certainly can't be super terrific, and there are ways of making sure (even if you don't chuck your pillows out every three months or so) that the buggers aren't overstaying their welcome for an opportunity to mess with your energy.

While it doesn't do any good to spend your time overly concerned about the various micro-critters making up your Universe (that shit will drive you crazy!), just like the seeds on the floor and the hairs in the coffee cups and the poopy-smell from the cat box, the critters you don't see, when running rampant, can truly upset your psyche with their little micro-pods of energy gluck — so you gotta think about this stuff a little bit, but not a whole lot.

So don't go all goofy on yourself! (By the way, if you've checked the gas knobs on the stove fifteen times in the last five minutes or blinked twenty-seven times every time you read the word "poop", you might want to get yourself some real serious professional help before you start messing with the microbes too much!)

As the journey to being a Spiritual Slob is about discovery, you may have noticed by now that I don't spend a whole lot of time spelling things out for you like you're some mother-tossing dummy. Us Slobs have intelligence — it's just that we're often too busy or stubborn or oblivious or paranoid to truly engage in our immediate surroundings, and of course, that shit's about to change.

So once you start examining your world, it will become obvious to you that that spack on the inner roof of the closed-in cat box did not come with the whole assembly when you bought it; that that dog of yours who hasn't been washed for four months is kind of unhappy and fuckin' stinks; and that that month's-old crusty stuff on the parrot's perch is not really supposed to be there, and suchlike.

If you use your eyes and your mind and your senses and search up and down and all around, just like one of those squiggly images that looks at first like somebody threw up their spaghetti on a board but is actually a picture of Jesus, it will all become perfectly clear.

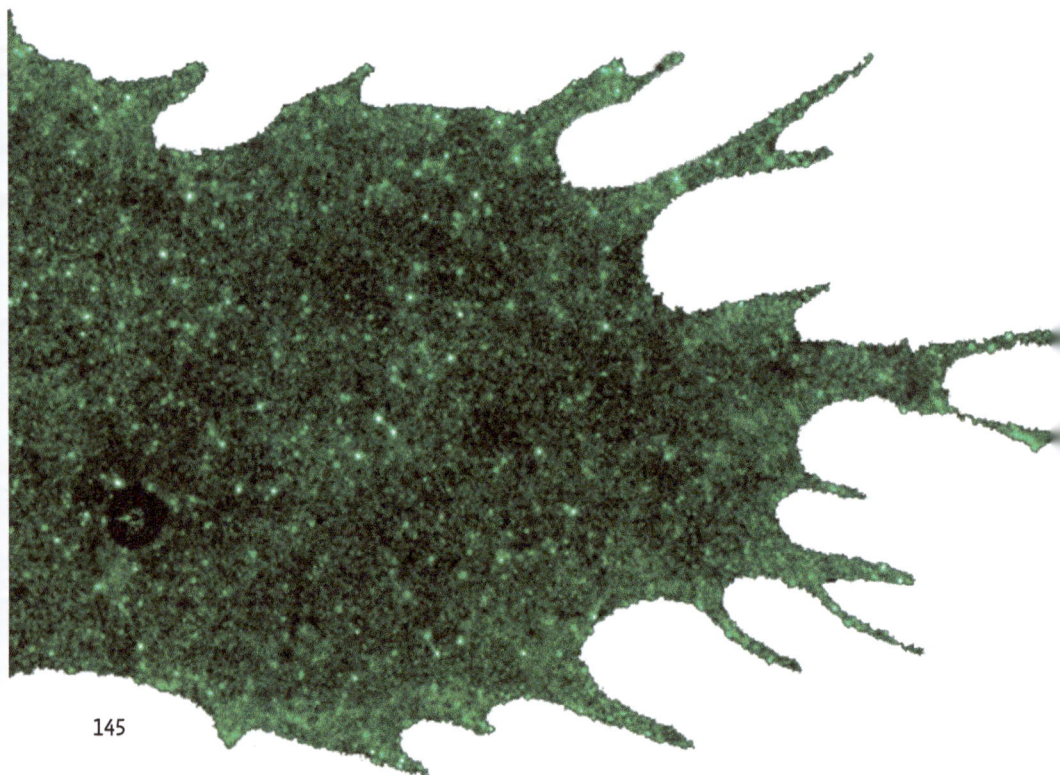

DROP YOUR DRAWERS AND TRIM YOUR BUSH

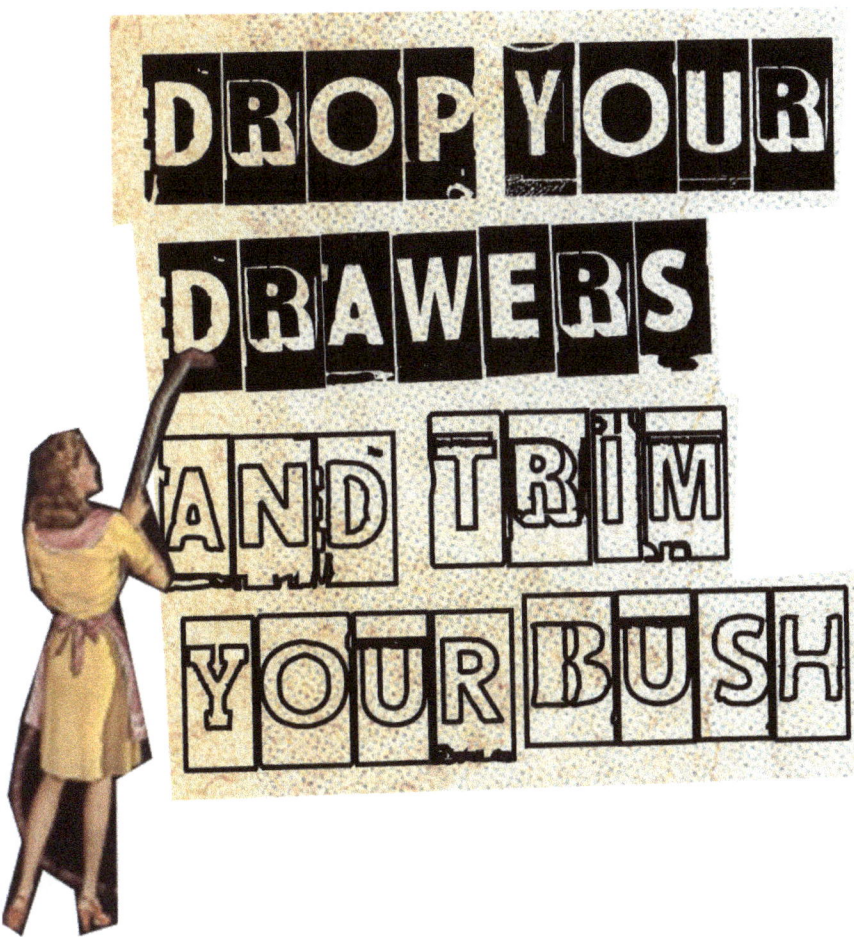

All those bits hovering outside your front door or back door or side door — your balconies and footpaths and window ledges and (in my case) weed-ridden boat-launch areas (yeah!) — are way too much to tackle in depth at this juncture in time, being as this is meant to be an action-packed kick-starter of a book that encourages you to recognize and embrace and use your inner Slob.

But by now I have confidence in the fact that you know a little look-see around will make things pretty clear pretty fast, and if they aren't, well just get that Big Arse of yours down to the Garden Centre or the Supermarket (or better still keep it local — those little shops in our neighborhoods need to keep going otherwise it's all Psycho-Bland-World ahead of us, and no matter how many quaint little delicatessen sections and Ye Olde Style coffee sections and surprisingly well-stocked Organic sections and delightfully colorful Kiddy sections there are in the Big Chains, variety breeds individuality and choice, and individuality and choice is what us Slobs are all about, Babies!!!), pull out some supplies and products, and toss them in your trolley and just get down to it!

Actually, for the sake of possible misinterpretation, I better add that you pay first, 'cos although a little devil in me finds the thought mildly amusing, I'm not prepared to write *The Spiritual Slob In Prison,* cause I may be a smart-ass, but I'm not a bad-ass and only advocate the most honorable of movements through this world.

Meanwhile, whatever aisle you do find that Arse of yours standing in, remember that everything around you is a mini-Big-Bang of mind and motion. I, myself, being a well-intentioned but often hypocritical-despite-myself Slob — lacking an immaculate carbon-footprint and very often the willpower to take even my own impeccable Virgoan advice — in fact do more than once in a while take a trip to one of the bigger Supermarkets when I'm in America and just stand, gazing at the condiment section and sucking up the sheer energy of choice and abundance and delicious consumerism standing before me, shelf upon shelf looming over me like a Warhol painting on crack, and even though they've ditched the only brand of brown sauce worth a damn in favor of the pale-tasting rubbish of their own Superchain's version, I can't help but be in awe of creation.

I love the fact that there are people sitting around design tables all around the world agreeing that they absolutely must put onto the market some cheap pig-shaped speakers (which I have!) or those weirdly printed gay-guy underpants with penis padding (which I don't have!) or coffee cups with dumb sayings (like "I'm a Spiritual Slob!") or yet another style of hot sauce.

I stand weeping at the beauty and complexity and overwhelmingness of this universe of supermarkets and small markets and confusing, unexpected carbon footprints and vegetation mixed with cow DNA and the sheer choices we have to navigate from Day One to Day Dot, when we pack it all up and go off to other adventures. And I weep at the relief of knowing that all I have to do to be the perfectly imperfect being I was meant to be is to march to the right aisle, scoop up a bunch of stuff, and get home to weed and pull and scrape and scour at the speed and intent with which I'm prepared to do it, which in itself is a massive meditation far more effective than dreaming of lotus flowers and shit like that.

So while I'm not gonna enter into the world of the Spiritual Slob Garden in detail (yet), I will tell you that if you decide to trim your hedge in the shape of a pig like I did recently, and the pig looks like it's missing one leg and has some massive facial deformity and an over-fat body and a withered, sickly looking tail, it's probably not doing the energy of your world a lot of good, and best just be left in all its glorious bush-ness until you speak to one another and agree on which way you, the bush, and your hedge-trimmers, can best combine your talents.

You might have guessed by now that I've only clustered together the would-be subjects of gardening and your drawers for the sake of the personal hilarity of the title, and by now you know and have accepted that that's the kind of guy I am, taking my freefall of ideas and advice in the same manner as that slipstream in which our lives unfold and the world whirls around us.

However, on a very tentative link concerning vegetation, I will reveal that only two days ago my good friend Sabrina texted me to reveal she'd discovered a runner bean in her brassiere. (I've yet to ask her if she was actually wearing the brassiere at the time, which would take it to a whole other dimension.)

Amusing though it might be to imagine her walking about town unaware that a not-insignificantly-sized vegetable was rustling about inside her delicates, I can only think that it instead found its way into her knicker drawer. (Don't ask me how — I have an imagination large enough to write a whole book about the possible various journeys a runner bean could make in order to find its way into a brassiere but not the stamina to bother right now.) I'd say that a good rummage through your drawers from time to time is an absolute necessity and sometimes, such as last week when I found a £20 note crumpled up amongst my socks, rewarding in ways you didn't even expect.

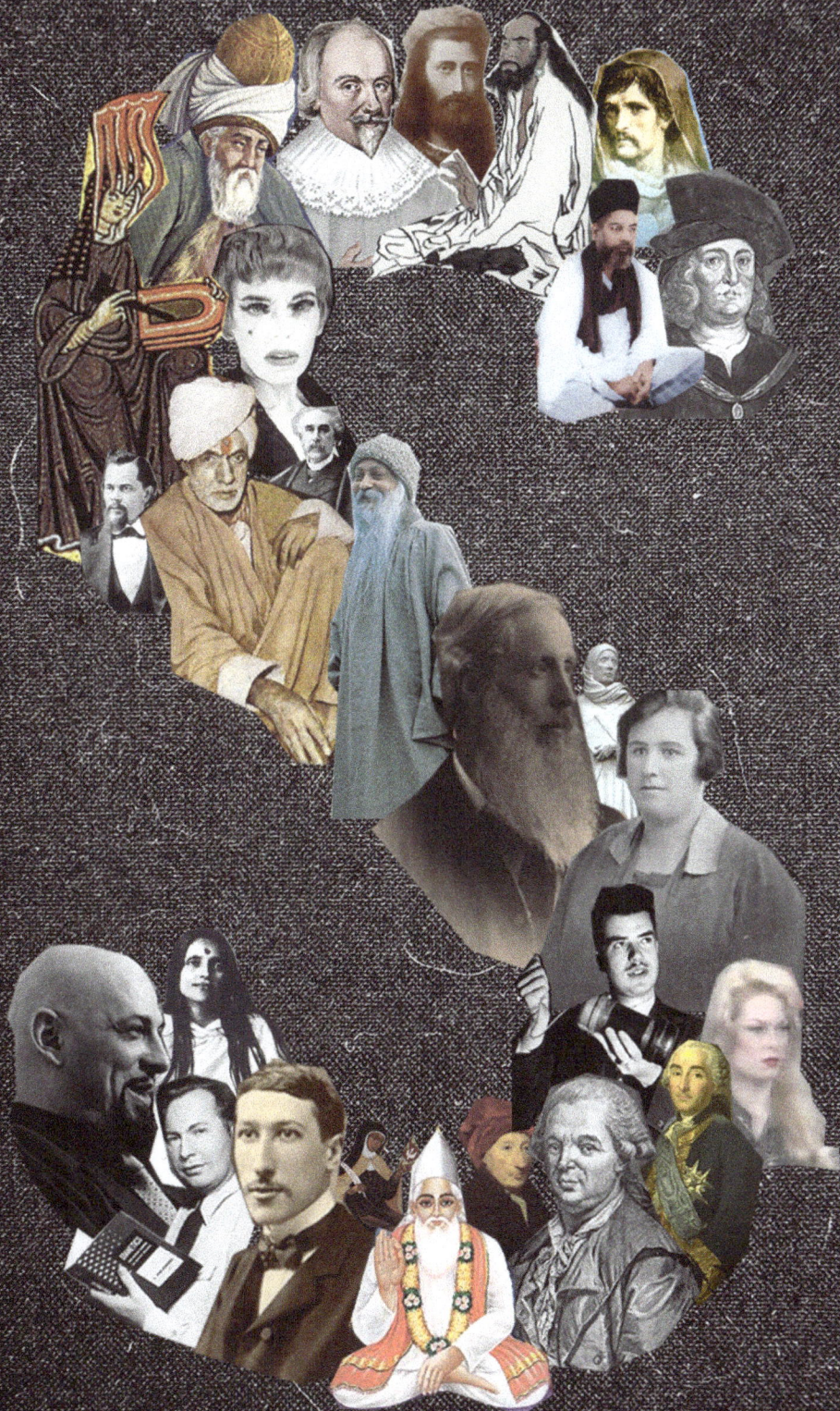

I cast my mind back to the beginning of this journey into Spiritual Slob-dom, to those dismal, dismantled offices and the drawers of their once-workers and now-displaced mystery beings whose personalities and energies could be deciphered like Mesopotamian cuneiform in a putrid potpourri of scrunched and layered and festering and melted items.

As with these ghostly personas, there is always that one drawer with everything shoved inside, waiting for future never-moments when all those things find their true places and functions that in actuality do not exist. We pretend, in this action of shutting away, to be settling these things into a significant halfway house, like an Ellis Island for the dislocated — ready at some stage to be recognized, itemized and positioned, but never really doing anything other than piling up until the drawer sticks, forcing us to shuffle them about and spread things around so that other things can be shoved in there, awaiting their sentences.

Like a Petri dish full of potentially scary micro-organisms, drawers such as these can be the Pandora's Boxes that, instead of unleashing the nasties, actually set us free.

More often than not, getting rid of the little don't-know-where-they-come-from beads and gum containers with the single stick of not-so-fresh-anymore gum and the business cards of people you can't remember who the fuck they are and pens that don't work and staples and rubber bands and lip balm containers and crapola you don't recognize leads to unleashing a whole lot of random, bugging-you-in-the-back-of-your-brain rubbish.

You'll be surprised how liberating chucking three-quarters of that mulch is, although at first it can be an irritating and traumatizing action — one very often filled with self-doubt: "Did I just unwittingly chuck the most important business card that's ever been handed to me?" or "Will I discover that sort-of-looks-broken plastic thingy is the epicentral necessary hub of some other plastic thingy I've stashed somewhere else and can't remember where it is but really really need?" There's often a weird sense of inadequacy and guilt at not being able to quite pinpoint where these objects should have gone, and why you're still ignoring them.

But, in the end, the rule of thumb is: Unless it's delightfully ornamental or being significantly and truthfully saved for some pending special moment, it's useless shit that bogs you down like plankton lacking a Remora. And I've put that word in here without explanation so you have to pause now and look it up, and part of that is because this book is very dense, and you need a forced break from time to time, otherwise you just think you're picking up what I'm laying down (or not), and part of it is because I personally hate it when I have to look up a word in the middle of a sentence, and I have enough evil in me to have a giggle at being able to do that to you right now. (Though I promise it's my once-only time and I won't be getting my jollies that way again, and at any rate, we're almost done, so stick with me!)

A BIG FAT WIND-UP

I hope you've had a hoot, Mind-Hoovering the Universe of Wise-Cracking Wisdom I've laid out for you. It's been a blast writing the kind of book I'd like to read, the kind of savvy, no-bullshit-spirit-earth-based stuff I think there should be a lot more of, cause after all, we've chosen to be on this orb and Life's too precious to spend it wallowing in a mire of aphorisms we've heard before, and sometimes the scent of jasmine and fucking patchouli (now I could write a book on how much I hate that scent!) gets a bit overwhelming, and us Slobs just want some of that gutsy life-soaked stuff we've come here to experience!

One thing's absolutely certain: We are all gonna kick it one day — at least as far as the particular persona we've currently adopted is concerned — so sweating our process to the Godhead is kind of redundant, as we all get there in the end.

So enjoy the world and that environment you've created around you, cause sure as shit, you *are* the Godhead in your particular expression of it, and your duty is to *get* that — get who and what you are as mirrored around you — and to make your adventures as cool for yourself and others as possible while having the kind of experience that makes us all happy.

One thing that remains gob-smackingly clear to me is a simple truth that a lot of people on this planet seem to be oblivious to, and which I urge you to remember each and every millisecond of your life:

If you wouldn't want that shit to be happening to you, it's a no-brainer that you shouldn't be doing it to others.

While that's a slight aside (and by now you are used to it!), I want to kick you out the door by telling you that, in your journey to becoming the ultimate Spiritual Slob, not to beat yourself up if you find irksome bits you wish you didn't have or stuff in your environment you wish you hadn't or things reflected you didn't know about before that you kinda hoped you'd remain ignorant of.

It's all where you're at now, and you, like all of us, have a choice at every moment of your life — like now — to create the world you live in. So get to it!

My taxi driver, Jack, a happy, down-to-earth dude who always takes me to and from Heathrow, was driving Coco home from the airport the other day and paused in his conversation with her — the kind of deep pause that makes one lean closer, waiting in anticipation — and said: "Can I ask you a question about Gregg?"

Coco, expecting the usual query about vocation or sexual preference, said, "Sure, what?"

Jack, focusing his eyes on her in the rear-view mirror, finally flopped it on the table: "Does Gregg have Tourettes?"

She almost pissed herself, and so did I when I heard that. I didn't quite know whether it was something to examine or something to be proud of, but it was deliciously, delightfully amusing and reminded me that sometimes it's hard to determine exactly what it is or who it is we are and certainly even harder to imagine who we seem to be to others.

So enjoy who you are, make yourself the best of what that is — whatever the fuck that means — cause you may never really find that out. But you can have a lotta fun getting to the mysterious destination that never really arrives.

ZONE OUT! BUT NOT FOR LONG MUTHUFUKKAH!

Ok, so you just finished the book and wanna get started, but like all things new and unexplored — and because you really are essentially a lazy fucker — you want it kinda spelled out for you, at least "until it all becomes second nature," you say. But really in the back of your mind, you're just expecting to be spoon-fed a bunch of stuff you can check off your list and get on with Life.

And that's fine for now, cause none of us expect you to go from Slob to Spiritual Slob overnight — though that, in fact, is totally possible. But you've been having a blast pigging out for so long that you just wanna kid yourself for a little while longer into believing that reading yet another spiritual self-help book is enough to get you to where you wanna be, rather than taking action. And we'll just let that fake hilarious vision dance around in your noggin' for a short while longer, just for shits 'n giggles, cause that's where we all started this journey, but we're now way, way far away from where we started, aren't we!

So let me make this clear, cause I kinda feel we have this super-terrific no-bullshit relationship by now: By using what I've written on the page that follows as a checklist without applying much further thought and taking the minimal amount of interested action — though not totally a waste of your money (cause let's face it, this book's fucking funny and terrifically entertaining and visually so stimulating that even if you've cacked out every item you've optically scanned along the way, you're still gonna be a better person for it) — you ain't gonna get the kind of Universe-shifting miracle stuff you really want. And I kinda hope by now you've seen how much additional fun you can have playing the You-As-Your-World game, rather than the Let's-Fuck-Around-And-Do-Dick-All game, which you've been playing for far too long. And that, my friend, is exactly why our Universes have happily collide

So you walk towards your place, navigating your way like a deer in a shit-filled forest — the familiar pathway crawling in weeds that sprout from patches of bare dirt — trudging obliviously over bits of chewing gum wrappers and crap, and enter the building where the "WELCOME" on your doormat is worn so thin you can barely read it (not that the light bulb that's been burnt out overhead for a year helps).

You can't even tell your front door is smeared in dirt and dust, not to mention see the grease on the handle from that hamburger you chowed down as you entered the night before, as you turn the key in the lock, back and forth and back and forth cause it always sticks and some day you'll get around to that. And you enter to find the Wellies you never use scattered in mismatched pairs around the edges of the hallway (just in case you need them), and casting your eyes around, you only just now start to scan the parameters of your Universe, cause I told you to.

So what do you feel and smell and see as you check out:

THE KNOBS

SWITCHES

EDGES OF THE CARPETS

CRACKS

FLIES IN THE LIGHT FIXTURES

SHIT IN THE DRIER

DIRT ON THE TOP OF THE LAMPS

HANDLES

THAT METAL BIT ON THE BOTTOM OF THE OVEN

THE FAN ABOVE IT

SPACK ON THE CEILING

MOULD IN THE CORNER

CRUMBS IN THE DRAWERS

THE PISS STAINS BEHIND THE TOILET

THOSE OTHER STAINS

MAGAZINES YOU'LL NEVER READ

YOU DON'T KNOW WHAT THE HELL THEY ARE

THE BROKEN REMOTE

DIRT-ENCRUSTED TOPS OF EVERYTHING

GUNKED UP BOTTLES IN THE FRIDGE

AND WHATEVER THAT IS WAAAAAAAY BACK INSIDE IT

You scan all of this, along with the other burnt-out light bulbs and cobwebs and rainspattered windows and weed-filled windowboxes and items you don't like and have never bothered to throw out and don't even see anymore along with the clothes that don't fit and never will again and cushions that itch even though they look good and pieces of furniture that are annoying but functional, sort of, and framed photographs of people you can barely stand anymore and things half-fixed you're gonna get back to the day after you die and stuff in drawers you don't know how to use, or don't work, and things you were given from people you love, though the things themselves you fuckin' hate...

Now take it all in, all of it. Remember that beer (or cup of tea if you're an AA/NA kinda person or simply hate the taste of beer!) you promised yourself at the beginning of the book? Crack it open now. Settle back and look around that wonderful world that has been, up until this moment, you — and reward yourself for the fact that even though you may not be right there, right now, it will very soon reflect the you you've always wanted to be.

Then roll up your sleeves and get down to it!

TANK U

Our stories, as alike or as different as they are from one another, invariably, like a Grimm's Fairy Tale, spill us into that enchanted malevolence of a forest with all its thorns and demons and weird, un-navigable, never-ending blackness that seems as if it can't help but destroy us.

And sometimes it does — in which case we never find out how the end of our particular story goes. But weirdly enough, most times it doesn't, and in burning us down to the ground it gives us a newness of insight we couldn't have claimed until we were slashed away from the bullshit we'd been carrying with us.

The characters in my story, those who gave me enough light to see me through my own haunted segment, are heroes of Love without whose existence I might just have, in a fit of self-flagellation and pity, been stupid enough to erase the scrawls of my subsequent chapters. And though I thank the many friends and family who brought me back, shuddering and stunned, to the other side of my tale, I'd like to particularly illuminate here the Reitz family, my Hands-On Uber-Champions of Light, who really got me through it all.

THANKS gang, I LOVE YOU ALL.

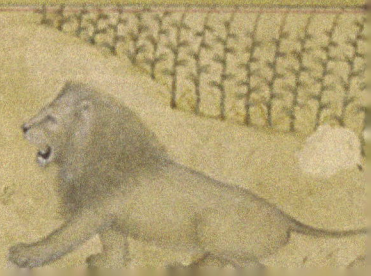

ABOUT THE AUTHOR

Whisked from the jaws of Kodiak bears by militant back-packing pirates on a rare Arctic spree, baby Masuak was eventually shunted off to a remote tourist attraction near Alice Springs to spend his childhood playing out various versions of the Bigfoot Myth, living on popcorn and the Wichiti Grubs tossed to him in pity for the poor display.

Perhaps it was this first venture into cheap entertainment, combined with an inherent propensity for personal transformation, that enticed Masuak one evening, in the middle of an increasingly disinterested performance, to set fire to his highly flammable ape suit and, in the distraction that ensued, teach himself to drive a stick-shift across the bumpy desert roads to Sydney, where the sharing of a crumbling squat with a myriad of male prostitutes aided Masuak in his Higher Purpose by the mastery of such key phrases as "Harder!" "Faster!" and "Ooh baby, you got it!", subsequently launching his job as a director (though fortunately those tapes were confiscated and vaulted, the whereabouts of which to this very day are still unknown).

With the persuasive side of the law urging him to new horizons, Masuak emerged from a rough wooden crate shipped across the Atlantic by local "exporters" and passed through immigration, using various tricks learned within the previously-mentioned squat, only to find himself at last in the place he was destined for: the throbbing conflicted egocentric world of English Civilization.

With the skills of a lifetime firmly held between two increasingly hairy but now vaguely deodorized armpits, Masuak whipped into shape such icons of the music scene as Kylie and the Spice Girls, showed uber-babes like Penelope Cruz how to shake their follicles, and with such heady fame throbbing in his veins, this wayward Sasquatch-playing bear-child has molded his creative tools in a vagabond way from the screen to the dazzling footlights of the theatrical world — the very stuff of his eclectic life.

Having spread himself across the globe like a two-penny whore, Masuak's vision now turns to more personal fish in the creative frying pan in order to make a difference in others' lives and to create entertainment that keeps us engaged in this Wicky Wacky World.

While some of this may be less than true, one thing is unshakably real, and that's Masuak's dedication to not just the art of Life, but the art of Thriving in Life — a skill he intends on relentlessly pounding into your very essence.

ABOUT THE ARTIST

Some say the city of Constantinople was the result of designs tossed away in angry dissatisfaction at the age of two by Emir Çaka Erkaya, and that after that the elusive genius-artist was held under lock and key by jealous artisans in a secret crypt beneath the city, for the next 800 years.

Finding this subterranean encasement less a punishment than an opportunity to hone his interior visions in the comfort of darkness, Erkaya's subsequent and undesired release by the Crusaders found him above ground but still shunning the light of day, forming a subculture of equally nocturnal artistic denizens that resulted in his unsubstantiated reputation as Vampire King — a title that has to this day generated the fear and secrecy this gloomy-ish Prince of Would-Be-Darkness requires in order to continue the honing of his beloved craft.

Managing to hold the world at arm's distance through the triad planets of Art, Illustration and Design, Erkaya has become a consummate master of his field and remains the undisputed international champion of Blindfolded Billiards.

www.ingramcontent.com/pod-product-compliance
Lightning Source LLC
Chambersburg PA
CBHW050822090426
42738CB00020B/3453

* 9 7 8 1 9 4 4 0 6 8 1 5 8 *